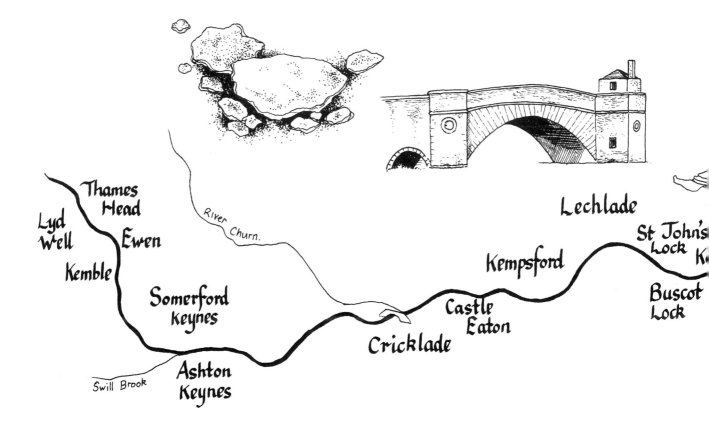

Lyd
Well

Thames
Head

Ewen

Kemble

Somerford
keynes

River Churn.

Swill Brook

Ashton
Keynes

Cricklade

Castle
Eaton

Kempsford

Lechlade

St John's
Lock

Buscot
Lock

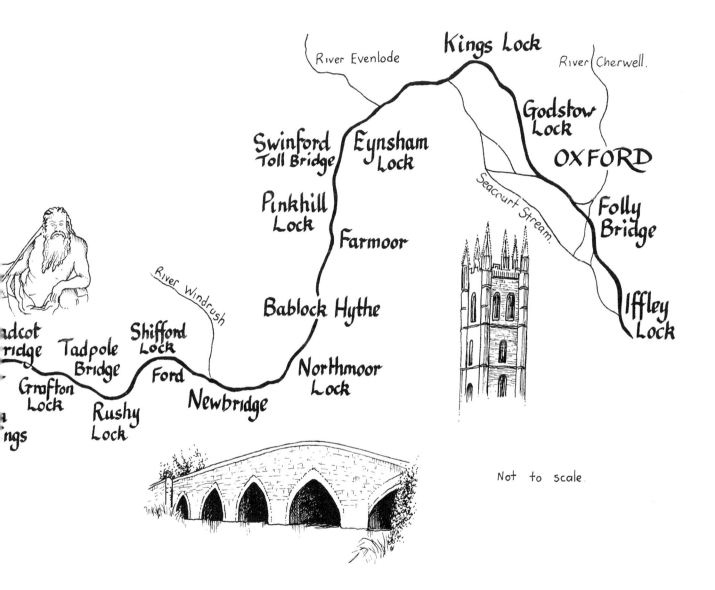

River Evenlode

Kings Lock

River Cherwell.

Swinford
Toll Bridge

Eynsham
Lock

Godstow
Lock

OXFORD

Pinkhill
Lock

Farmoor

Seacourt Stream.

Folly
Bridge

River Windrush

Bablock Hythe

Iffley
Lock

dcot
ridge

Tadpole
Bridge

Shifford
Lock

Grafton
Lock

Ford

Northmoor
Lock

ngs

Rushy
Lock

Newbridge

Not to scale.

THE STRIPLING THAMES

Also by Mollie Harris

A Kind of Magic
Another Kind of Magic
The Green Years
The Archers Country Cookbook
Country Cooking from Pebble Mill
From Acre End
A Drop O' Wine
Cotswold Privies
The Magic of the Cotswold Way
The Cotswold Country Cookbook
Where the Windrush Flows
Wychwood: The Secret Cotswold Forest
Privies Galore
Country Wines: To Make, Drink and Cook with
Village Christmases

THE STRIPLING THAMES

From the Source to Oxford
with
MOLLIE HARRIS

Illustrations
GARY WOODLEY

ALAN SUTTON PUBLISHING LIMITED

First published in the United Kingdom in 1994
Alan Sutton Publishing Ltd · Phoenix Mill · Far Thrupp · Stroud
Gloucestershire

First published in the United States of America in 1994
Alan Sutton Publishing Inc. · 83 Washington Street · Dover · NH 03820

British Library Cataloguing-in-Publication Data

A catalogue record for this book is available from the British Library.

ISBN 0–7509–0403–8

Library of Congress Cataloging-in-Publication Data applied for.

Typeset in 13/18 pt Garamond.
Typesetting and origination by
Alan Sutton Publishing Limited.
Colour separation by
Yeo Valley Reproductions.
Printed in Great Britain by
Bath Press Colourbooks, Glasgow.

Contents

CONTENTS

Mute swan with cygnets

Artist's Preface

In 1989, having completed *Where the Windrush Flows* both Mollie (the author) and myself were preparing to launch the book. A few weeks before the publication date I was invited by a close friend, Antonio Vasconcellos, to attend his 26th birthday party, which was being held on board *The Marchioness*. I was looking forward to seeing my friends who had recently moved to London. But I didn't get to the party; I cancelled the taxi, pleading fatigue.

The rest is history, but I lost four close friends that night. I had met them a few years earlier in Oxford, where *our* journey on the Thames has ended. Sadly, at the book launch for *Windrush* those familiar faces were absent.

Now, with the publication of the Thames book, certain stretches of the river seem to bring back the memories of that tragedy. But, like the river itself, life goes on.

There were days of storm and days of peace that floated over the river. Like Mollie says in the book, it began with pouring rain and ended with rain, but to me there were many happy sunny days that will always mirror the friends I lost.

GARY WOODLEY

Acknowledgements

All along the Thames I have met with lots of folk who have readily chattered to me about the river.

I would especially like to thank Mick Bowl, Derek Bloomfield, Colin Budden, Tim Brown, Reg Coole, Mrs Carter, Julie Cockburn, Molly Cooke, Nick Elwes, John Florey, Sandra and Denis Fairall, Leigh Fenton, Miss P. Gauntlett, The Hon. Mrs Ann Gascoigne, Mrs I. Harris, Yvonne Keeble, Peter Kellard, Wilf Loader, Graham Margeson, Mr McCreadie, Ron May, Mrs Sainsbury, Ken Smith, Tony Sargent, Tom Stanier, Bob Williams, John Wilmer and Robert Willis. All these – and *many* others – have helped to make my journey along the stripling Thames more enjoyable, and indeed unforgettable, for which I thank them.

My main source of information came from a small booklet called *Tales of Ales*, written and researched by Michael Lewis and Roger Marks. There are also snippets from several booklets in churches that I visited along the way.

MOLLIE HARRIS

The Stripling Thames

Rising in a valley meadow
Shaded by a giant Ash tree,
This infant stream
Meanders through those early villages –
Ewen, Coates, Kemble and Summerford Keynes.
This bubbling stream, soon to gather strength
Before reaching Cricklade, Castle Eaton and Kempsford.
Then on to Lechlade and St John's lock –
Where 'Old Father Thames', reigns over the widening water.
Tumbling on to Radcot bridge,
Where many a battle was won and lost.
Lovely names and lonely spots, like
Tadpole, Rushy lock, Chimney and Shifford,
Where King Alfred held his first parliament.
Old Newbridge, Northmoor, and Bablockhythe,
With memories of 'The Scholar Gypsy'.
Pinkhill, Swinford, Eynsham, and skirting Wytham Woods –
Under a canopy of oak and beech.
Then to King's lock, an easy reach, and on to Godstow,
Where Fair Rosamond won the heart of a King.
Next to lonely Binsey church and Saint Frideswide's well –
And Port Meadow where cattle are grazing, nearby to Tumbling bay.
Too soon to Osney, where once a famous abbey stood;
Then on to Folly Bridge, where the infant Thames becomes of age,
And where strong young undergrads become 'Head of The River'.

Mollie Harris

A winter scene: birth of the Thames

Introduction

The stripling Thames, which rises at Trewsbury Mead in the parish of Coates, near Cirencester, and just north of the Fosse Way, has been a favourite study of folk over many many years, and obviously several well-known writers have produced books about it.

So, to be able to write a book about this famous river, at least the first forty miles of it, has been for me a labour of love and a great joy. I have seen new places, revisited old familiar ones, and delved into the details and history along the way; throughout my journey I have found most people very kind and helpful.

In its infancy the Thames flows past the villages of Ewen and Coates, murmuring music as it meanders along those first few miles. But too soon it flows through more villages and hamlets spoiled only by huge areas of water, lakes and pits – where millions of tons of gravel has been, and still is being, extracted. Someone once said that the area was like 'the gold rush of the Ucon'; to the owners of the gravel pits, yes, but not to the immediate villages around.

The Thames Valley has always attracted settlers, and there are still traces of when Neolithic man discovered that fertile valley. Much, much later, the Romans came and stayed for 300 years. They withdrew in the fourth century, but not before they had shown the nation a different way of life, building their great straight roads, vast villas, and introducing a culture that has never been equalled. After they left our shores, along came the Saxons and the Danes and, much later, the Normans, all with their different ways of life which gradually changed the lives of the Thames-side dwellers and indeed most of Great Britain. And when they finally departed our shores, they left behind their lovely churches, castles and crosses.

So the land surrounding the noblest of rivers has played a very important part in history, as the river flows under old stone bridges, past lofty country mansions, through flat, flower-filled meadows, where cows and sheep 'safely graze', past stone-built villages and small towns, through many locks and weirs and lush pasture land, enriching the landscape, and helping to make the surrounding countryside a great attraction to us all.

Much later, the rich land owners came to Thames-side, building wonderful country mansions, with great gardens and parks, some surrounded by miles of stone walls. These gentry employed a number of local people, both to work in their great houses and in the gardens and farmland which surrounded their vast estates. They entertained royalty and the like, and for many years they lived off the fat of the land. Some of those big houses still remain, beautifully maintained.

The river at one time played an important part in the lives of the folk who, with their boats and barges, brought food and wood, stone and many other commodities to the people who lived on its banks. These folk have now gone, but in their day they were often the only link and lifeline along some of the more remote places along the river. While the roads and byways at that particular time were in a disastrous condition, so the River Thames became a very busy 'highway'.

These days the river is mostly used for pleasure and much is being done to help people to enjoy the amenities. Boats are bigger and more luxurious; at Folly Bridge in Oxford, Salters big pleasure boats, all newly painted, await the summer season. All along the river some of the old bridges and Rights of Way are now being dealt with. There is a big discussion going on at the moment about the proposed very 'modern' footbridge that the Countryside Commission hopes to build at 'Bloomers Hole', just below Lechlade. This will restore an old crossing over the Thames, linking the tow-path on both sides of the river which would be useful when the long-distance path, starting at the source, at Thames Head in Gloucestershire, and ending at the Thames barrier in London, comes to fruition – hopefully either this year or the next. Then there are more suggestions for the renewal of old bridges, and already some have been replaced by the National Rivers Authority – one at Ten Foot Bridge, near Tadpole, and further down-river at Old Man's Bridge. There are plans to build a new footbridge at Shifford, and the Field Paths Association are pressing the County Council to rebuild a footbridge that was a Right of Way at Skinner's Bridge – a bridge which the people of Farmoor and Eynsham used quite a lot.

The proposed Thames path, which the Countryside Commission hopes will follow the original tow-path wherever possible, has recently met with a few problems. For one thing, upstream from Lechlade there wasn't ever a tow-path – but no doubt the planners will get over that somehow. But what a wonderful thing it will be when the path is finally opened, when hundreds – indeed thousands – of people will be able to follow the route, and walkers and ramblers will find peace, and sometimes total isolation, for miles, discovering the beauty of the river-side throughout the changing seasons, and the wildlife, trees and flowers which are our very heritage.

Old water pump: 'Those were the days'

It must have been one of the foulest days of January when I set out to find the source of the River Thames. When I left my home in Eynsham, it was mizzling with rain and the forecast wasn't good, but this was the only day that I could spare. The journey of some forty miles took me through one of the loveliest areas in the Cotswolds, and despite the grey day and the leafless trees, some colour at least came from yellow dancing catkins on the hazel bushes, and the gently undulating hills looked very beautiful. There were vast brown fields, ploughed and tidy, waiting to be planted, while others were already green — because of all the rain we had had — with autumn-sown barley and wheat showing well. Several flocks of sheep, who didn't seem to mind the wind and rain, were busily cropping the quite lush green meadows.

I was making for Cirencester, and then on to take the A429 towards Tetbury, but I had to look out for a sign to Coates or Ewen. Through the rain, which in the strong wind was literally blowing horizontally across the sky, I saw a sign to Ewen. Not really knowing exactly where the 'Thames' source was, I stopped at two cottages hoping to find out a little about the place, but there was no one at home in either of them. I drove on down to the village, going first under a now defunct railway bridge, but on this awful day the place seemed deserted. So, I turned the car around to make my way back to the main road. Then along the village road came a middle-aged lady riding her bike, struggling against the nasty wind and rain. 'Best ask her where the Thames' head is', I thought.

'Excuse me,' I said, 'sorry to trouble you on such an awful day, but could you tell me where to find the source of the Thames?'

She jumped off her bike and answered in the kindest, most polite manner.

'Yes, madam. Of course, madam. You need to go back under the railway bridge and then on to the main road again. Turn right, madam, and then sharp left, along the road a little way, and that will bring you on to the village of Coates. Then ask there madam.'

I thanked her very much.

'It's been a pleasure to talk to you, madam', she replied, and mounting her bike, rode off, head down against the elements.

Following her instructions I soon arrived in the village of Coates – not a soul to be seen, and who could blame folk for staying indoors today of all days! Then, coming down the drive of a big stone-built house, I saw a red Post Office van. 'Ah', I thought, 'here's someone who will know.' Stopping his van beside me, a young, cheerful-looking man, said, 'Yes, dear, can I help you?'

'Please', I replied, almost pleading, 'could you direct me to the source of the Thames?'

'Oh yes', he said. 'Mind you, I've never seen it, and I've lived round here all my life, but I've been asked several times as to where it is. Now', he went on, 'turn around, take the first turn on the right; after about two miles you'll come to a railway bridge {it was not the one I'd been under before} and almost immediately you will see a turning to your right. A sign will say "The Tunnel House Inn", it's up there somewhere, they'll tell you at the pub.'

I reached the pub sign, and took the right hand turn. It was a private road and not very well maintained. Talk about the 'rocky road to Dublin'! it was full of pot-holes and swimming with water. After a while I reached the

Tunnel House Inn, which was first built for the navvies and other workers to live in when the Thames and Severn Canal was built in the late eighteenth century; later bargemen were also housed there. Then, when the canal ceased working it became the inn it is today. The deep gully which runs alongside the road is the remains of that canal.

I got out of the car, knocked on the front door, wandered around to the back and knocked again – but no sign of humans, only the barking of dogs both inside and outside the pub. I'd almost given up hope, then thought I'd try once more on the front door. A woman's voice called out, 'What do you want?'

I told her that I'd been advised to come here, and that I would be told where the source of the Thames was. She unlocked the door, holding a large dog by his collar.

'He won't hurt', she assured me. 'Come in.'

I introduced myself.

'I'm Pam', she said cheerfully.

Then a man came into the room, it was Chris Kite – *mine host* of the inn.

'She wants to know the way to the Thames' source', Pam told him.

'Go back to the village, where you will see a footpath sign to your right. Take that and walk over three or four fields, and you'll come to it. That's Trewsbury Mead', he said.

I thanked them very much, saying with a laugh that I'd probably return – but not before 'the sun shines both sides of the hedges'.

By now I must have looked like a drowned rat, and they probably thought I needed my head read to be out on a day like this.

'I hope you've got some wellingtons', Pam said.

'Yes', I replied, 'in the car.'

So, with their straight-forward instructions, I at last found the footpath sign that would eventually take me to the source. I parked the

Two centuries-old stone stiles

car on the grass verge. The stile over to the field was one of those solid stone slab type, with two stone uprights let into the Cotswold wall. The lichen on the stone slab showed up yellow and almost luminous in the gathering gloom. The stone foot-rest, where countless numbers of feet had stood, was worn away to quite a hollow. This was a Right of Way footpath to the village of Ewen. The field was surrounded by a Cotswold drystone wall, which was in excellent condition. With the weather still blowing and raining, I set off, determined to find the source of the Thames. A little way along the path there were two or three sections of wattle-fencing, stood up against the wall; most likely the farmer had used them to pen some sheep in at some time. Wattle-fencing is an extremely ancient craft, much older even than Cotswold stone walling. Back in the reign of Queen Boudicca and the Iceni tribe in about AD 60, wattle-and-daub fencing was used to build huts for folk to live in and also to make pens to keep cattle in.

A large flock of rooks was busy feeding in a field of grass; most likely they were finding plenty of worms and grubs that had come to the surface because of flooding.

I plodded on, crossing over yet another lovely stone stile. I slipped and slithered in the muddy water – you could hardly make out where the path began and ended. The next two stiles over Cotswold stone walls were of the wooden ladder type – evidently erected either by ramblers or the local council. They were very well made, with three or four steps on each side, but of course not as lovely as those made of ancient stone slabs. I passed a field of

Rooks busy feeding on grubs

swedes and turnips, their tops all pink and shiny in the wet; some had been washed out of the soil and were floating about.

When I was young, we children often pulled up swedes and turnips from the fields, gnawing off the roots, tops and skin, and then eagerly eating the raw vegetables – lovely they were, too.

Once, a local farmer, Mr Parker, caught me pinching a swede. Now, my mother had always drummed into us that if we were caught doing anything we shouldn't, we were not to run away but to stand our ground. So I stood there watching Mr Parker's long thin legs getting nearer and nearer, his face purple with rage.

'What du think you're doing, then?' he bellowed.

'Just eating a swede', I answered timidly.

'Well', he said, shouting loudly, 'you tell your stepfather I want to see him [this was the farmer for whom my stepfather did some weekend work]. And if you don't tell him that I want to see him, I shall let him know that I caught you pinching.'

I never did tell him – I knew that I would get a hiding from my mother for pinching anyway, and I don't think that Mr Parker – for all his threats – ever split on me either.

A little while ago I read in a book that just a hundred years before this incident with Mr Parker, a young lad of sixteen was sent to jail for a month for stealing turnips. Good job that sort of punishment didn't exist in the days of my youth!

But I didn't stop to pinch one this time – probably because I was not so hungry as I used to be in those hard-up days of my childhood.

In the distance I could see that the next field was flooded like a lake. 'If this isn't it', I thought, 'I'm off back home!'

Reaching the middle of the field, I could see a stone pillar away to my left. I splashed through the

In the beginning: water bubbling up through stones

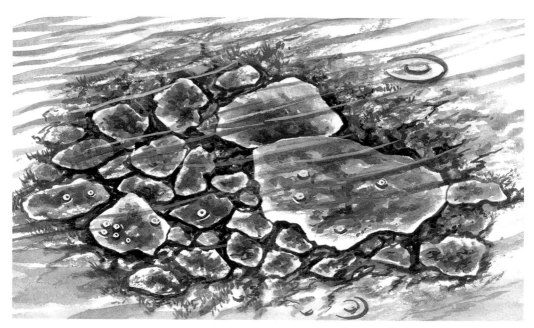

Source of the river

quite deep, fast-flowing clear water, and reached the pillar. Looking down into the water, there it was, a few feet away – the source of the Thames! It was under water, but clear to see, a circle of stones some 3 or 4 feet across, with water bubbling up from somewhere. At last, I'd reached my goal for today. I read the chiselled out words – now quite faint – on the stone pillar:

> The Conservators of the River Thames 1857–1974
> This stone was placed here to mark the source of the River Thames.

At one time there was, in fact, a stone statue of Old Father Thames here, but it was removed to St John's lock, near Lechlade, some years ago for fear of being vandalized in this lonely spot. And growing beside and quite near to the water's edge was the biggest, tallest ash tree I have ever seen – it was at least 80–100 feet high; perhaps this, too, was planted to 'mark the spot'.

A bright cock chaffinch

It was still raining and blowing like billy-oh, but my step was light (despite the mud and water) on my way back to the roadway. Quite a large flock of chaffinches and goldfinches rose up from a hawthorn bush in front of me, twittering and flying in loops. But the rooks that I had seen earlier had undoubtedly moved on. On this day I had planned to visit Somerford Keynes and Ashton Keynes, but I was wet, cold and tired after my trudge across those flooded fields. But I was also feeling quite triumphant – like the explorers of old! I had pushed on, overcome the hazardous weather, searched for, and found my goal!

Another week passed before I had the chance to visit the valley of the stripling Thames again. Thankfully the day was dry, but with a biting, pesky north-east wind blowing – the sort that doesn't go round, but through you. First I made my way to Cirencester. Besides wanting to have a look at this lovely town I needed to check something in the library. The magnificent parish church, which stands in the centre dominating this busy and interesting town, is a lovely Cotswold stone building holding many treasures. 'Tis no wonder that the Romans made this their second most important city, with long straight main roads leading to London and other important places. Names like Fosse Way, Ermin Way, and Akeman Street are still used today. This was a fine Roman city, with public buildings, wide streets, baths and an amphitheatre, a very wealthy place in fact. The Romans left in AD 400.

During the Middle Ages Cirencester became an important centre for the wool trade with cloth-making and weaving much in evidence. Then, centuries later, the Severn Canal reached the town in 1789, bringing goods from far afield. Today both the canal and the old railway line are no more.

On this cold – beastly cold – day I thought I might find a local person to have a chat with, but shoppers were scurrying home to the warmth of their houses, heads down against the icy blasts that were rushing up the streets.

So I took the road which led to Kemble. I stopped and thought I'd look in at the church, but the door was locked and once again there was no one about to ask. Having read the delightful book called *Kemble, Ewen and Poole Keynes* (three villages on the infant Thames),

Lovely old stone bridge

published in 1992 and written by someone who lives there, I think that anything I write would be superfluous. So I took the winding country road to Somerford Keynes.

First, I came to a lovely stone bridge over a river. This, I thought, must be the Thames. It was quite wide and rushing along as clear as clear. The river was much wider here – the reason being that between here and the source, three or four more springs join the Thames. In a copse-like wood which ran alongside the river, I could see a well-worn, much used, muddy pathway. I wandered along the path for about a quarter of a mile. It was pleasant walking along there – the trees sheltering me from the biting wind. The river twisted and turned several times, rushing around the sharp bends making small whirlpools and creating bubbling eddies as it did so. There wasn't much wildlife or activity along there, only the clear swirling river. I did notice that the dark shiny leaves of the lords and ladies were already showing under the trees, and just before I reached the bridge an almost chestnut-coloured Jenny Wren flew across my path to the other side of the river, where it settled and scratched about on the verge, almost dancing on the wet mud.

Over the road, in a field, an inquisitive dapple-grey horse stood and stared. As youngsters living in the village of Ducklington, if ever we

The river at Ashton Keynes

The stone bridge at Ashton Keynes

met a dapple-grey horse coming along the road, we quickly licked our forefingers and made a cross on the toe-cap of our boots or shoes, and on no account would we dare to catch sight of its tail. I never found out the meaning of this ritual – probably lost in the mists of time – but we children would not have missed carrying this out for whatever the reason.

This was definitely not a day to dilly-dally, so I made my way to the next village of Ashton Keynes. All the way there I saw miles and miles of huge lakes where gravel extraction had taken place – no doubt a haven for wildlife, but there wasn't much evidence of this on such an extremely cold day. Somewhere in this area, two of these vast lakes have been turned into Keynes Country Park, where folk can sail, picnic, fish and windsurf. There is also a children's playground and nature reserve.

I reached Ashton Keynes. Almost in front of me was what I thought was the village pond. So I walked along a small road to my left, edged by a narrowish, quiet, slow-moving stream. At the end of this road, from under a narrow bridge, water came suddenly tumbling and bubbling. A lady living nearby stopped to chat.

'Is this the Thames?' I asked.

'Oh yes', she replied. 'Just here where the water gushes through is much photographed.' She went on, 'If you go up this dirt path by the side of my cottage, you'll see the river is much wider up there.'

I took her advice and was surprised by the quiet and slow-moving river – so different from when I had seen it at Somerford Keynes.

I turned back and retraced my steps, back almost to where I had parked the car. In front of me was an ancient cross, one of four that are standing in different parts of the village. I walked over a little bridge where the river took a sharp turn to the right, leaving what I thought was a pond on my left. Here, the Thames flowed alongside the High Road, where there were several houses. Each one had a delightful small bridge leading to it from across the river, making it a very attractive road. I wandered back to my starting point, and noticed a sign down a lane to Church Walk.

A little way along there, around a garden, were a number of upright stone slabs joined together by small iron clasps. These clasps were probably the work of the village blacksmith many moons ago. This unusual form of fencing made a most attractive enclosure around two sides of the garden, and were probably as old as some of those lovely stone crosses erected in the village.

The Church of the Holy Cross further along the lane was restored around 1877, although there are still parts which are of the Norman and Perpendicular periods.

Looking at a signpost, I saw that Cricklade – which will be my next port of call – was but a few miles away. But my visit there will have to wait for another day, and the chapter for February.

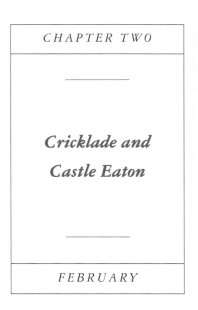

It was a cold, cloudy day when I made my first journey to Cricklade and the surrounding area. The weather wasn't typical for February. I suppose we'd had our 'fill the dyke' weather in January – evidently the wettest for many years.

Along the roadside hedges, among the bare trees and bushes, the lovely willows glowed, their branches ranging from amber and gold to red, a very welcome sight on this cold drab day. Long before I reached Cricklade – the only Wiltshire town on the River Thames – the beautiful tower and pinnacles of St Sampson's church rose up above the town and surrounding meadows.

After parking the car – it's a *free* car-park – I wandered down the wide and very pleasant street, passing close to the lovely St Sampson's church (so-named after a Celtic bishop). At the junction of the High Street and Calcutt Street, stands a tall, elegant clock, painted dark green, gold and red. The time can be seen from three sides of the clock, though thankfully for the old clock winder, the workings have now been electrified. On a plaque it states: 'In commemoration of Her Majesty Queen Victoria, 60 years reign, 1897'. In the High Street there is a very good variety of shops that seem to cater for most of the needs of the inhabitants. People were popping in and out of the shops doing their shopping – from the butchers, bakers, grocers and many others. You name it, Cricklade has it. In fact, Cricklade High Street reminded me of how several of the high streets and towns that I have known *used* to look

Old clock in the High Street, Cricklade, Wiltshire

Winter rabbit

in the past. I do so hope that the people of this charming town will be able to maintain this friendly homely feeling.

Castle Eaton church with its unusual bell tower

Passing St Mary's church and right down at the bottom of the main street, I noticed that there were neat stacks of sandbags outside some of the low-lying cottages, but I learned later that – thankfully – they didn't have to be used.

Near here, on its way from Cirencester, Ermin Street – one of the great Roman roads – passes quite near to the town, and in fact continues along the nearby bypass.

Finally, I reached the Thames, and wandered along its side in a nearby meadow. From one of the drunken willow trees that border the river, a great spotted woodpecker flew. The only reason that I could think of why he should be there was that perhaps he was after the ivy berries, small bushes of which were growing in the centre of the willows where other birds had left seeds. Somewhere near here, in 878, King Alfred crossed the river to fight the Danes. He also fortified the town

Lovely great spotted woodpecker

Castle Eaton from the river looking over to St Mary's church

by building an earthen rampart which, centuries later, was replaced by a high stone and timbered wall. Also close by is the River Churn which flows into the Thames just before reaching Cricklade.

Back up the High Street I called at the Council Office and spoke to Yvonne Keeble, the Town Clerk, who was most helpful and gave me a booklet about the town and a most useful leaflet on the famous North Meadow where the fritillaries grow. But all this will have to wait for another day when I hope the weather will be less unpleasant.

Two weeks had passed since my last journey to Cricklade. The weather was still dry but, thankfully, there was now quite a lot of sunshine to warm things up a bit. Around the countryside things were stirring, birds, now with mates, were rushing about, and here and there in the hedgerows blackthorn blossom was blooming, and occasionally an early maybush was already showing green shoots – 'bread and cheese' we called these when we were young, and greedily ate those fresh green leaves. Suddenly, in the grass, I saw one of the first of the wild flowers blooming – a mass of bright yellow coltsfoot. We, as children, called them 'pee the beds', and were afraid to pick them – just in case!

Today I'd made arrangements to meet 73-year-old Reg Coole, a man who was born in Cricklade and, I was told, a mine of information – and I was not disappointed! Among the things he told me was the fact that between the tenth and twelfth centuries AD, there was a royal mint at Cricklade, and that during its working time, coins were minted before, during and after the Norman Conquest. Over sixty of the Cricklade coins are known to still exist, and some have been found in Sweden, where apparently they had been used for tax purposes, known as 'Danegeld'.

Mr Coole is, in fact, a High Court Bailiff, a very ancient office of the Cricklade Hundred and Borough and Mr Ralph Neeld is the Lord of the Manor. The court meets every two years and although they haven't the powers that they had many years ago (now much of it is controlled by the Parish Council), there is still an Ale Taster, a Constable, a Carner (meat) and a Scavenger (who was responsible for the roads' upkeep) and a Hayward (for grass etc.), especially for the 109 acres of the North Meadow. This meadow, bounded on the north-western side by the River Churn and on the south by the River Thames, is a nature reserve which preserves the fritillaries (snake's-heads) that grow there in their thousands in late springtime. Experts say that one of the reasons why these flowers grow there so prolifically on the banks of the Thames – and indeed at my old home too, at Ducklington on the River Windrush – is the flooding in wintertime, which brings all sorts of deposits, plus the gravel base of the meadows. This mixture is just what the fritillaries need. These days, the meadows are carefully grazed – grass is cut but with no sprays or fertilizers added, leaving the fritillaries to bloom and multiply. And, of course, no picking is allowed as they are now protected, but when we were young, we children used to go and gather them by the armful. I can still picture the high school window ledge with rows of jam jars simply stuffed with them, mostly still in bud and *really* looking like snakes' heads.

Four years ago a boat carrying one ton of cargo made its way up the Thames from Oxford to Cricklade. This was really to keep the Right of Way of boats on the river, and also to keep it navigable. Just outside the town there is a place on the Thames called Hatchetts, where, many years ago, baptisms were performed by members of the local Baptist chapel. Mr Coole also told me that quite a lot of poaching took place at one time, and how the old fellows would 'tickle the trout' to catch them. No doubt the fish made good nourishing meals for the hard-up families. One old character, Mr Coole told me about, was Tuney Harvey, who slept rough in old barns. He would stand in the street and sing just to get a few coppers for beer. And in the season for

The moss-covered roof over the old lych-gate at Castle Eaton

Long-tailed tits and spring catkins

watercress — which for the wild variety is only when there is an R in the month — Tuney would gather some and then sell it in the town.

In Cricklade there is still a glove factory. Apparently at one time there were two working in the town. When I came down the High Street I noticed a window full of lovely gloves, which the factory make.

'Is the river used much by the local people?' I asked Mr Coole.

'No, not like it used to be. As children, dozens of us used to paddle and swim in it all through the summer holidays, at a place just along the way, called Eisey. Sometimes parents would come, too, and picnic there. It was lovely. Before the war, Reverend Claud Tickell was vicar for Eisey and Latton, and to get to the Eisey church he had to walk over the fields. This he didn't like doing because of spoiling the wild flowers or killing insects. So he and his wife used to turn up for the services in daps — what we call plimsoles.'

As I walked across into the car-park, I noticed a dozen black-headed gulls perching on the roof of a building. They were all sitting quietly, in a line, and all facing the same way. I stood for a moment looking at them. An elderly man was crossing the car-park and stopped to chat.

'I'll bet you be wondering what they be doing up there all facing the same way?' he said.

'Yes, I did wonder', I replied.

'Well', he said, 'you can always tell which way the wind is blowing — just look at the birds perching, they allus sits facing the wind.'

'Why is that?' I enquired.

''Cos they don't like the wind up their ass, that's why', he said, as he walked off, chuckling.

Well, it's time I left this charming town and made my way to Castle Eaton a few miles away.

After leaving the bypass I took the winding road through Water Eaton and soon reached Castle Eaton. Near the church I met a man pushing a small modern lawnmower.

'Hello', I said, 'going to be busy?'

'Well, it's nice and dry, so I thought I'd cut the grass round my wife's grave', he replied.

'Have you lived here long?' I asked.

'Ah, a few years now. 'Course, like everywhere else the village has altered, but not as much as some places, thank goodness.'

I noticed an old water pump in the nearby hedge.

'Some time since that was used, I'll bet', I remarked.

'Yes, I can't remember just when we was put on the water, but I do remember seeing the women with their buckets meeting here, and there was another pump near the school. Good job them days be gone when the women had to fetch every drop of water from these old pumps.'

Then quite suddenly he wished me good-day and went through the lovely lych-gate and up the wide path to the church.

I made my way to Manor Farm where I understood I could get the key from Mrs Sainsbury, so that I could get inside the church. St Mary the Virgin stands on the bank of the Thames; in fact, the churchyard runs right down to the river bank. The church has evidence of the Norman period still visible in the north and south doorways. The building is beautifully cared for. What struck me was the wonderful assortment of hand-worked, richly coloured kneelers – these alone speak of the love, attention and dedication of the congregation to the church. Outside, apart from the lovely square tower, St Mary's is very different from any other church for it has a Sanctus Turret on the roof, complete with a bell inside it, which dates back to early Catholic times. For many years the bell was kept inside the church and was used as a ting-tang bell. In 1900 it was restored to the turret. Then in 1961 – because of age and damage – the Sanctus bell Turret was dismantled and rebuilt, and the bell rehung – back again where it belonged after it had been banished for more than three hundred years.

Well, the month of March came in like a lion, with very cold north-easterly winds and some night frosts – 'blackthorn winter' is what my granny used to call this time of the year. 'We allus gets cold east winds when the blackthorn blooms', and she was right, for it was blooming in the hedgerows, looking like snow on the otherwise bare branches.

But within four or five days the wind had veered around to the south, the sun came out and suddenly, so did the hedgerows, bringing a bit of colour into the countryside. There were early hawthorn bushes, green and beautiful, and glorious trees of pussy willow, their branches covered with yellow fluffy buds, like so many day-old chicks. And suddenly the horse-chestnut leaf buds were bursting out on the topmost branches. On my way to the Thames side there were thousands of dancing daffodils, golden forsythia, pink prunus and almond blossom in the country gardens, glorying in the sudden spring sunshine. The old 'uns will say, 'We shall have to pay for this!', or that it 'is a weather breeder'. Whether it is either of them or not, nobody seems bothered, the sunshine makes everyone look and feel much happier.

Today I saw my first dandelion blooming. Within the next few weeks the verge sides will be massed with them. I shall be making some dandelion wine and some dandelion tea. The tea is supposed to do wonders for the complexion, and is very health-giving. The wine, if kept for a few years, is more like whisky. There were also masses of celandines, shining and sparkling in the grass like hundreds of golden stars.

The lovely old church in the village of Inglesham

Today I was making for the village of Kempsford. Many, many years ago it was called Knyemersforde – 'The ford of the great marsh'. Today Kempsford is a small quiet village – apart from the frequent noise of the aeroplanes that fly from nearby Fairford and Brize Norton. Centuries ago quite a number of noblemen lived here, one of whom was John-of-Gaunt, who married Blanche of Kempsford, a descendant of the Duke of Lancaster. They lived in a castle on the banks of the Thames there. And, although it was King Edward the Confessor who built the first church

Bells of St John the Baptist

here, it was John-of-Gaunt who built the beautiful tower, around 1390–9, in memory of his first wife, the Lady Blanche. As you enter the north porch of St Mary the Virgin, notice the horseshoe nailed to the door. According to historians, the first Duke of Lancaster's only son was drowned in the ford there. The Duke was so griefstricken and overwhelmed that he rode like mad out of the village, never to return! As his horse galloped away, it lost a shoe, which was picked up and nailed to the church door where it still remains to this day.

But now I must make my way to Inglesham, the next village on my way along the Thames. Inglesham is a gem of a place, peaceful and quietly remote. The old church of St John the Baptist was locked; I understand that it was made redundant in 1979, but is cared for now by the Redundant Churches Fund. I noticed that the old door had fairly recently been lovingly repaired, and I could see the old bell turret on the roof, with its two bells looking out towards the river.

However, there had been no sign as yet of Inglesham's famous round-house, which I hoped to visit, so I enquired at one of the lovely Cotswold stone houses nearby.

'Ah! T'is over there, over the fields', the lady said, pointing. 'First you'll have to go across a field, then you'll come to a little wooden bridge, you'll see it among some trees away to your left. 'Course', she added, 'You could reach it from the road, but I think you would enjoy the walk across the fields, over another field and you'll come to a big bridge, go over that and you soon come to the round-house.'

So I set off, thankful that it was a fine sunny day – windy, but quite pleasant. As I neared the round-house the river seemed suddenly very wide. It is somewhere near here that the River Coln joins the Thames along with the remains of the canal. This must be a favourite spot for wildlife – I counted no less than forty-two Canada geese, either resting or cropping on the bank, four pairs of mute swans, and a solitary black one. There were also several moorhens, coots and wild ducks; and one proud mallard, with a green velvet head and neck, swam along majestically with his dutiful nondescript wife following behind. There is a reason for the females' lack of colour. A bit further on by the riverside was a flat bunch of dried reeds. I stood and gazed down on what I would have thought was a nesting place, but for the moment the area appeared empty. Then a slight movement caught my eye; it was a female duck sitting tight on her nest — wonderfully camouflaged by her nondescript plumage.

Inglesham round-house

At last I reached the famous round-house, now a private dwelling, but there was no one at home there, or at the house nearby. Round-houses were built to accommodate the lock-keepers and length men. They have three rooms — one above the other, with a spiral staircase built into the thickened wall on one side which holds the fireplace and flues. Apparently four of these unique houses still exist between Inglesham and Sapperton on the old canal route.

Miniature houses at St John's lock

Round-house and cottage at Inglesham

I turned around and made my way back over the fields to Inglesham village. On the way a solitary heron flew up clumsily and sailed off across the sky. Larks were singing high above, and under my feet was the new green grass of spring, speckled with daisies.

'Time I made my way to Lechlade', I thought. Lechlade takes its name from the tributary, Leach or Lech, which joins the Thames nearby. It is a busy bustling town, with the stately church of St Lawrence dominating the square. It is one of the great wool churches and its prominent spire is a landmark that can be seen for many miles around. Turning right from the

Lechlade church from the Thames

church I made my way to Halfpenny Toll Bridge, named after the toll which had to be paid to cross over it. The bridge was built in 1792 and has one big centre arch with two smaller ones at the sides, and the toll house is still there.

Lechlade was once a very busy trading place along with the river and the canal, and there were several wharfs on the banks where produce from the surrounding countryside was stored before being sent off downstream to

London. Now it is a favourite place to moor your motor boat in this delightful countryside.

A bit further down the road by the river-side is a well-marked and well-kept picnic site. I remember coming here years ago when my eldest grandson was camping with the cubs. From there I could see St John's lock away over the fields, but my best plan would be to drive there.

St John's lock is a lovely tranquil place, but not for much longer as the lock-keeper, Bob Williams, told me. 'We shall start getting busy at Easter and from then on it's all go until late autumn.' The lock, the first on the

Thames, was ablaze with early spring flowers. The lawns had been newly cut, and nestling among the shrubs were two or three delightful tiny stone houses. Bob Williams told me that an earlier lock-keeper had made them for his children when they were small. And there, in all his glory, was the dominant figure of Old Father Thames, lounging in the sunshine. This huge stone figure was commissioned by R. Montie for the Crystal Palace Exhibition of 1851. Around the figure and also in stone are wool bales and a

Halfpenny Toll Bridge at Lechlade

barrel. In 1958 it was presented by H. Scott Freeman, Esq., a conservator of the River Thames. It was placed at the head of the Thames, at Trewsbury Mead in Gloucestershire, where it stayed until 1974, when it was moved by the Thames conservancy, for fear of vandalism, to St John's lock. But more of how the operation went will be revealed in the Eynsham chapter later on in this book.

The 'old man' himself, Father Thames, at St John's lock

CHAPTER FOUR

*'Oh, to be in
England
Now that April's
there'*

ROBERT BROWNING

APRIL

In April the weather often takes one step forward and two backwards. Early this month we had some quite cold days, then suddenly the wind changed and we had a warm, sunny day – but the day after, it was back to the cold wet winds again. Despite this the countryside had begun to look lovely, the colours were simply beautiful. The leaves of the poplar and oak trees were almost pink – a soft, pinky fawn, and the hawthorn bushes were massed with that lovely new green, which unfortunately only lasts a little while before it turns dark green for the rest of the season. There were so many different shades of green on the trees and hedgerows, all blending perfectly. But the blackthorn blossom, so startlingly white last month, had now turned to a dirty grey – and as I passed a thick hedge, the petals scattered my path like confetti.

The spring-planted corn was already a delicate green sheen on the brown fields. What a truly wonderful time of the year! Each spring I think that this one is better than the last.

I reached Buscot, which is a National Trust village. The verge sides were delicately embroidered with primroses and violets. At the entrance to the main street stands a substantial village hall and clock tower, which was built around 1890. Nearby there is an ornate-covered well, but with a water pipe and tap; years ago, of course, it would have been a hand-operated pump. This, and some of the stone cottages, were built by the first Lord Faringdon who did much for the village during his lifetime there.

The one-time village water supply at Buscot

Buscot today seems a quiet, peaceful place, though no doubt when the motor cruisers come up the Thames things will liven up a bit. I called a couple of times during this month, but saw very few people. The little village shop was well stocked and the post office is housed in a room at the village pub, The Apple Tree (although the pub part is now closed). The village houses, apart from those on the main street, seem to be dotted about away from the centre — even the church and the old rectory are some way away.

I visited the church of St Mary, a lovely peaceful place where I spoke to an old fellow who was walking past. I remarked how quiet the village was with no one about.

'Ah', he said, 'All the old interestin' 'uns be in there', nodding in the direction of the churchyard.

'Nowadays', he went on, 'You don't know many of the folk what lives here . . . I'd rather talk to that old bull out there!'

And, believe it or not, when I made my way towards Buscot lock sometime later, blow me if he wasn't in the field with the bull! Who was it who said, 'there's none so queer as folk'?

The village has not always been so quiet. Edward Lovenen Townsend, who built Buscot House around 1780, was also a very successful farmer. He and his staff produced cheese in great quantities which was shipped from a warehouse at Buscot, known as The Cheese Wharf, down the Thames to London. Then, in 1859, the house and the huge estate was bought by a rich Australian called Robert Campbell, a very go-ahead gentleman who brought with him farming methods that were extremely modern for the time. One thing he did was to plant fields of sugar beet from which, in a huge building on a spot called Brandy Island, he extracted sugar which was then exported to France and apparently used in the manufacturing of brandy.

While I was in the village I heard about a new footbridge that is to be built over the Thames at Bloomers Hole, which lies between Lechlade and

Buscot. It will be a bridge especially for walkers and will take the place of an old ferry which used to link one side of the river to the other along a tow-path on the northern side. The bridge, when it is finally built, will form a vital link on the 200-mile Thames path from the source in Gloucestershire – which I have already written about in the first chapter – to the Thames barrier in London. The bridge was designed by Cezary Bednarski and will be a beautifully simple arch, and will be – to use his own words – 'like a blade of grass bent over the river'. It will be the first bridge in Europe to be built of carbon fibre, a new revolutionary material developed in Great Britain, with a clear glass balustrade.

Path to the privy at Kelmscot

The cost of such a wonderful bridge is estimated to be around £140,000 and building will hopefully start later on this year although I was unable to find out from the Countryside Commission when the work will be completed.

The villagers of Buscot, however, are against the construction of such a modern-looking bridge.

Three-hole privy of Kelmscot Manor

There is a very informative booklet called *A Historical stroll around Buscot*, which you can buy from the friendly lock-keeper. It is full of interesting facts about the village and its past.

It is time I made my way to Kelmscot, a few miles away.

Buscot lock

Kelmscot Manor was the home for twenty-five years of William Morris, the writer, artist, craftsman, poet, printer and reformer, who lived there with his beautiful wife from 1871 until his death in 1896, and is buried in the churchyard of St George's church. The artist, Gabriel Rossetti, also lived there for some time with them.

William Morris loved the Thames and the meadows surrounding his home, and once wrote, 'Kelmscot has come to me to be the type of the pleasant places of the earth, and of the homes of harmless simple people not overburdened with the intricacies of life, and as others love the race of man through their lovers or their children, so I love the earth through that small space of it.'

A visit to Kelmscot Manor is a MUST (it is open every Wednesday from April until September). It is full of Morris's life's work — wonderful tapestries, carpets, paintings and materials. The house is set in lovely gardens and even has a super 'three-holer' privy in the garden, which, of course, must have

The beautiful stone summer-house in the garden at Kelmscot Manor

Kelmscot Manor House: no wonder Morris loved living there

been used in Morris's lifetime. One can imagine he, Rossetti, and Burne Jones – another artist who stayed there for some time – all sitting together in a row, discussing the day's events, for it was not unusual in those days for folk to go to such places together and chat!

The house and grounds are so peaceful and beautifully maintained that the visitor comes away refreshed and calmed, with a reminder of an age now gone.

Today, as April draws to a close, the verge sides are massed with dandelions, buttercups and cow parsley (called kek in my neck of the woods), and some of the fields are brilliant yellow with acres of oil seed rape. The dazzling colour reminds me of the lemonade powder we used to buy as children. For a halfpenny you got a small scoopful in a three-cornered bag, such a treat it was! Goodness only knows what was put in it to make it so yellow, as one young lad remarked, 'It makes yu pee green.'

The birds are so busy just now, rushing about, building houses and feeding their young. There are blackbirds, chaffinches and yellowhammers – to name just a few – and nearby I heard those few magical notes of a cuckoo on the last day in April. Back at home in Eynsham, high in a tree, a mizzle thrush – also called a northern thrush, a storm cock and wet-headed thrush – sings from sun-up until sun-down.

For the first nine or ten days of this month strong, very cold, north-easterly winds did – as Shakespeare wrote – 'shake the darling buds of May', although the sun shone all day, and out of the wind and in 'the burro' it was quite warm.

But, despite the cold winds, the countryside looked lovely, and to use one poet's words, spring was 'all of a rush of richness . . . miles of lush, green meadows and hedgerows'. On my way to Radcot Bridge, which was my next stop on the Thames, I saw copses and woods full of the beautiful purply-blue of clouds of bluebells.

CHAPTER FIVE

'Where black-winged swallows haunt the glittering Thames'

MATTHEW ARNOLD

MAY

The may, or hawthorn bushes, were fully out – masses and masses of sweet-smelling blossoms (which make a delightful white wine). The blooms on the horse chestnut trees were also wide out. As children we always called them 'Whitsuntide candles', for that is what they look like – giant candles in beautiful green candlesticks. This year they are out at least two weeks earlier than usual.

Many of the other trees were showing young leaves. The oak and the ash were vying with each other as to which could come out first. I think the oak was just ahead which means, if we are to believe the old country rhyme, that we shall have a dry summer:

> The oak before the ash, we shall only get a splash,
> The ash before the oak, we're bound to have a soak.

Wartime bunker and may tree

In the low-lying Thames-side meadows, brilliant golden king cups or marsh marigolds show up in the 'standing grass' – an old-fashioned name for grass being grown for hay, or these days for silage; and cuckoo flowers, or ladies' smocks, sweet-smelling cowslips and bitter sorrel – which we used to eat as youngsters – speckled the long grass. The cow parsley, with its frilly lacy flowers dancing along the grass verges, was hedge high in places.

On reaching Radcot Bridge, I saw dozens and dozens of black-winged swallows, and several swifts and martins – all busy building their nests under the lovely stone bridges there. The coming of these migrants means that summer is really on its way. There were also dozens of river craft dotted along the river-side. No doubt their owners have been busy getting them ready for the coming summer.

There are two stone bridges over the Thames at Radcot, with a continuous flow of traffic crossing them. One of them is, in fact, the oldest bridge over the river; built of Cotswold stone, it was erected in either 1229 or 1312 – different historians give a different date. Whichever it is, there was an even older bridge there in about 958. Unfortunately, this lovely old stone bridge with its three arches was not wide enough for the loaded barges to go under, so in 1787 another one – very near to the first – was built. The old one still has the Thames flowing under it, while under the newer one is a navigable channel along which boats – and also a long-boat – glide up to Lechlade and beyond.

This is a lovely stretch of the countryside, and can be viewed at leisure, especially if you take a beautiful, slow ride on the long-boat *Battersea*. When it reaches Buscot lock, the owner's wife says its time to put the kettle on and, when I made the trip a little while back, the passengers were offered welcome cups of tea. There is a break at Lechlade, with time to have a look around the town or have a meal, and then the delightful ride back begins, past all sorts of river wildlife and herds of contented cows grazing in the flower-filled meadows. The pilot – for that, I suppose, is what he is called – gives an interesting commentary about the places of interest – which, of course, includes William Morris's Kelmscot. Here, much to our delight, we made a stop, and I walked once again up the farm track to view the lovely Cotswold stone house and its surroundings loved by Morris for so long.

I had arranged to call and chat to the hosts of the Swan Inn at Radcot – Sandra and Denis Fairall, who have been here for three and a half years. Before that they kept a pub in Uxbridge, but when they heard that Morlands were looking for new tenants at The Swan it only took one look at the inn and its lovely surroundings, and the Fairalls were hooked. Today it is a cosy, warm, inviting place, with the main decoration on the wall being a wonderful display of stuffed fish, caught thereabouts. The taxidermist, I learned, was a Mr J.W. Cooper, who himself caught and stuffed a wonderful pike in 1958. You can tell which of the fish are his handiwork, for all his frames have a gold border.

While we were chatting, the Fairall's two dogs – German schnauzers called Cambric and Lace – fussed around and one insisted on sitting on my lap while I tried to take notes. A very different reception from when I first met them outside – good guard dogs, I would think. The day

Green woodpecker

'Where black-winged swallows haunt the glittering Thames'

The first old bridge at Radcot

Swan Inn

The old meeting house

before, Sandra told me, she had baked several rook pies for a group of Inner-Wheelers' luncheon meeting. This is a spring delicacy, as only the breasts of young rooks are used. These young birds were shot by Denis and a farmer friend.

The menu for lunchtime and evening meals looked very appetizing, and several folk dropped in for food while I was there.

Outside there's a lovely walled garden, just by the river-side, where on warm sunny days folk have their afternoon teas, and sit and watch the wildlife or boats pass by. Round the back there is a strange-looking stone building, and Sandra told me that one of the old worthies had suggested that it might be part of an old chapel at one time. There is another stone building which is still called the toll house – although no actual tolls were ever collected there. But many years ago, when the barges came from upriver loaded with Cotswold stone (for St Paul's), and cheeses, fruits and other products, it was here that goods were transferred on to larger vessels and then taken to London. In that little toll house was the man who paid the bargees for their load of goods, which they had brought from upstream. The men then probably retired to the pub to spend some of their hard-earned money.

As we were chatting in the yard a solitary rook flew slowly overhead – 'There's one that got away', I said to her, laughingly. Gary, the artist for this book, who was with me on that day, said that his father used to shoot young rooks, and that his mother had also made lovely pies with them. He also said that his father had once shot a heron, and being glad of some extra meat at that time his mother had plucked and cooked it – 'It was horrible!' he said. 'A bony, fishy, old thing.'

Having written about the nicer things around Radcot, I mustn't forget to mention that history recalls that more than one battle was fought there – it being an important crossing over the Thames. Richard II fought Henry Bolingbroke there in 1387, when the bridge was greatly damaged, and during the Civil War, when Oxford was held by the Royalists, there were battles and skirmishes for possession of Radcot Bridge.

Before I made my way home, I thought I'd call on John Willmer at nearby Friars Court, Clanfield, whose farmland skirts the Thames. John Willmer is one of the leading conservationists in the county – a

The one that got away

very likeable man with brilliant ideas about the future of farming and the land. The government's set-aside scheme is already working on his farm. He and four other farmers have started working on a wood, fuel and energy project, each on his own farm. The first plantings of new coppices took place in the spring, under the Woodland Grant Scheme. John Willmer took me to where the new willows are being grown for this work, but all along his land, which skirts the Thames, there are old established willows growing. I was also shown a wondrous machine which, when fed with willow branches – NOT great thick ones – these emerge as fine wood chips. Of course, a good steady market has to be found for the use of the wood chips.

But Friars Court is not just a wood-growing farm, there is much more of interest there. I was taken on a super nature trail, including a lakeland area which attracts wildlife of every sort, and meadows with cattle grazing in

Cuckoos calling, a sound we all long to hear

Song thrush

The Battersea: 'take a slow boat' to Lechlade

them. This trail is open from April to October. At the end of the nature walk there is a very nice tearoom — cream teas and ploughman's lunches and lots of other interesting food served in what was the old back kitchens — now beautifully decorated, but still containing the old original copper, pump and bread ovens.

Well, after a very full day I think it is time to wend my way home, and plan the next stage of my walk along the stripling Thames.

For the first week of the month we had brilliant sunshine with temperatures up in the seventies – it was indeed 'Flaming June'. Late may blossom and cow parsley were still blooming, and the elderflower bushes were absolutely smothered and dripping with blossom (again this makes a lovely delicate white wine – and also the very popular elderflower champagne, which is a beautifully refreshing summer drink and very simply made).

One year, when I was at a Yorkshire literary luncheon, publicizing one of my books, the sweet was summer fruits served with a delicious elderflower cream. I made enquiries about it from the head chef, and he very kindly gave me the recipe – which was a great honour apparently.

The grass fields were yellow with buttercups and masses of moon daisies, meadowsweet and mallow graced the verge sides. There was a great variety of grasses, including meadow fescue, rye grass, cocksfoot, timothy and many others, shaking their pollen at the slightest breeze, while sprays of delicate dog roses climbed and draped themselves over the hedgerows. It was a truly lovely summer scene. In several fields, hay-making was in progress, some already completed with giant black plastic bales of hay waiting to be picked up. On one side of the road there was a field of bright yellow oil seed rape, and on the other a field of linseed, as delicate a blue as a summer sky. What would our fathers and grandfathers make of such crops and methods if they could see them now?

Wonderful reed warblers

The kingfisher, the jewel of the river

Field of golden rape, a familiar sight

As I walked along the private road that skirts the Thames all the way to Rushy lock, cuckoos called and reed warblers warbled in the tall green reeds at the edge of the river, and every so often there was the brilliant blue flash of a kingfisher. I hadn't arranged to meet the lock-keeper, but by the look of the river craft heading his way, I knew where I'd find him.

And it was a pleasure to meet the genial lock-keeper, Graham Margeson, who lives there with his wife and four children. They have been there for the past eight years. The lock was built in 1896, but the

Rushy lock: long ago the film stars' haunt, now the lock-keeper's house

weir was there much earlier, and last year, Graham told me, approximately 5,000 boats went through his lock from April until September. Some folk come up the river year after year, he told me, 'so you get to know them'. One party from Scotland often send him a haggis. Every now and then we had to break off our conversation as one boat after another came through. Across the river from where we were sitting, black-winged swallows dipped and flew. 'They are nesting in that garage and the shed over there', he said. 'I reckon when the swallows arrive that the weather's going to get better, and it's true,' he went on, 'ever since they came this year we've had some lovely days. Yes! it's a sign alright, I've noticed it time and time again.'

I remarked on the super building where he and his family live.

'Yes', he said, 'I was told that in the first place it was built as a shooting lodge and all sorts of famous people used to come down here and stay – and not just for the shooting by all accounts.'

Where Graham finds time to do his garden is a mystery, but both flowers and shrubs made a colourful display. But despite the amount of work he is very happy and contented to live in that quiet peaceful spot – well, peaceful, except for all the boats that go through! It's a hard job, too, turning the great wheels and opening the huge lock gates time and time again. By now it was mid-morning and things were hotting up a bit, so I took my leave and set off back down the private road leading to the country road. As I reached it, the Trout Inn at Tadpole loomed up. There used to be a cottage there – as well as the pub – but that is now in

The Trout at Tadpole

ruins. So now Tadpole is the smallest hamlet in England. The Trout is a fine stone building, and *mine host*, Mick Bowl, was watering his flower garden at the front of the inn. I asked him if he could spare a little while to talk to me about the place.

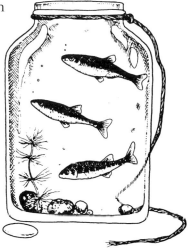

'You go and sit in the garden', he said. 'I'll get some coffee sent out for you, and I'll be with you in ten minutes.'

We settled ourselves in the beautifully kept garden and lawns which ran down to the Thames. Mick and his wife and children have been there for three years – prior to this he had been in the police force. The fishing rights which are in the hands of the landlord – in Mick's case the owner of the inn – goes from Rushy lock on one side to Ten Foot Bridge on the other, a matter of about three miles in all. Many fishermen come down from Birmingham and Coventry and spend the weekend or a day there. There is a huge camp and caravan site situated behind some trees. Many come for the coarse fishing, but some just come for the peace and tranquillity of the countryside. They do lunches and dinners at the Trout – rabbit pie, pigeon hot pot, rook casserole, and lots of other tempting dishes.

I noticed a fair sized chalet in the garden.

'What do you use that for?' I asked.

'Well, nowadays it's somewhere to keep the garden tools and lawn mower in, but at one time – before the fishermen had their own cars and caravans to stay in – some of them slept in there. Mind you', he went on, 'there was only one bed in there, which was soon confiscated and fifteen or twenty men just slept on the floor. Then, apparently at some time it was used as a mortuary. But if you want to know more about this place, the fellow you need to talk to is Wilf Loader. He lives at nearby Aston, and he's my right-hand man, and has helped at the Trout for many years.'

So Mick kindly gave Wilf a ring, and he said it would be alright if I called to see him the next day.

Meanwhile I was keen to walk along the river to Ten Foot Bridge, which is the end of Mick's fishing rights, and a matter of nearly two miles. The day was very hot with very little breeze. Along the river-side I saw some kingfishers – a wondrous fleeting glimpse of azure blue. There were also swans nesting, and several cows on the other side of the river were standing hock-high cooling themselves, while others were drinking – dipping their great heads into the water, then lifting them back again as the water cascaded from their mouths. On the bankside several of the herd stood in the shade of a big maybush.

I passed a huge plantation of mature poplar trees standing in straight lines obviously planted some time ago for a special reason. 'I must remember to ask Wilf Loader about them when I see him', I thought. I felt that I had walked miles and miles, but I still hadn't reached Ten Foot Bridge. The hot sun bore down relentlessly and I was very warm and weary so I turned tail and made my way back to the Trout – perhaps I'll be able to reach the bridge from the roadway some other time.

It was another lovely warm day as I drove over to the village of Aston. Wilf was standing by the door of his bungalow waiting for me. His garden around him was bright with summer flowers. He told me that he has been water bailiff on the Thames for forty-seven years, and still enjoys every minute of it.

''Course, conditions have altered since I started all them years ago', he told me. 'Back in the early days, all the land round Tadpole – including the Trout – belonged to the family of Wellesleys at

A kingfisher diving for food

Cows cooling their hocks

Buckland Manor and we used to poach hundreds of rabbits. Mind you, some farmers liked you to catch the rabbits because they did so much damage to the crops.'

'Did you sell the rabbits locally?' I asked.

'No, country folks knew how to catch their own. No, ours was to sell to the fishermen when they come down at the weekends in them charabancs. What we used to do was to catch the rabbits all the week, sometimes a hundred of 'em — and do you know how we kept 'em fresh? Well, we'd string 'em on ropes, like you strings onions, and then we hung them down one of the two wells that was out in the yard. The top of the wells was

On the way to Ten Foot Bridge

ground level and they had big wooden covers on 'em so's nobody could fall down 'um. The old policeman would come round looking for poachers. He'd stand on the wooden cover over the well and say "By jingo! if I could catch one o' them poachers, I'd soon have him up before the beat", not realizing that he was standing on the evidence! When the charabancs drew up, the men would pour off them, eager to buy the rabbits. We'd often get two and sixpence a piece of 'um.

'Years ago all the lighting in the pub was either tilly-lamps or candles, and if you wanted to get some bottles of beer from the bottle cellar you had to go through the ladies lav, shouting as you went "is anybody in there?"

'Then there was a police sergeant who used to call. He loved his beer and would sit down in the cellar supping and getting very tiddly, 'till he could hardly stand. At closing time, we'd sit him on his bike and lead him back all the way to Bampton.'

'Oh!' I said, 'what do you know about all those poplar trees that are growing along the Thames side?'

A rabbit

'Ah, they was planted – two thousand of them – by the landowner for Bryant and May, the match people, for the purpose of making matches. But after the first war cigarette lighters began to be fashionable and gradually the sales of matches went down, so the trees were never used.' He went on, 'And there they stands like regiments of soldiers. I don't know what will become of them.

'Mind you, we've had some funny and some sad things happen at Tadpole. Once a fellow went out in a canoe and it tipped over and he drowned. I dived in and tried to find him, but there's a few deep holes about where he went down and I reckon he was in one of them. So we called the fire brigade, and eventually they found him. Then, because at that time the middle of the bridge over the Thames was the boundary between Oxfordshire and Berkshire, there was a great argument with the police as to which was to make out the report – was he found in the Oxfordshire half, or Berkshire – now, of course, the whole bridge is in Oxfordshire.

What might have been

'One day I was walking along the river bank near the Trout when my nephew said, "Look, there's a cow in the river". And sure enough there was an animal in the water, but it was a bull not a cow. It was stuck in the mud with only its mouth and nose showing above the water line. I stripped off and dived in, but I couldn't budge it, so called to my nephew to go for a rope. Well, he got just round the bend, and a boat came along. He told them what was wrong. Thankfully they had a rope aboard, so I sat on the bull's back and threaded the rope through the ring in its nose, and together we managed to get the animal into the shallows. It was absolutely exhausted! So I runs over to Bampton for the fire brigade who got the poor animal out and it lay on the grass for a while, for it was nearly a gonner: it must have been struggling for hours. Well, eventually it got to its legs and very unsteady, walked off. Apparently it was a very valuable animal that belonged to a local farmer.'

Well, I think I could have written a book on Wilf himself – a remarkable man with such tales to tell, but I did want to make another call, so I thanked him and bade him goodbye.

According to my map, there is a small loop going from the Thames to Duxford, while the main river seemed to go straight on to Shifford lock. I needed to find out about this loop in the river so I called to talk to retired farmer, John Florey, who had farmed at Duxford for many years and still lives there in a delightful bungalow.

The reason for the loop, he said, was that at one time the Thames flowed that way. There is a big ford which existed there centuries before the Romans came to our shores, and which is made up of huge paving stones set in

Summer flower

the river. But, during the summer, the water was only a few inches deep and boats had to be hauled over the ford. So, in 1897, the Thames Conservancy decided to cut a new course which bypassed Duxford and made a new lock – the last new lock at Shifford. But the loop, with its quiet back-water, still remains.

Shifford lock, in the words of its lock-keeper, Derek Bloomfield, 'is miles from nowhere, nothing ever happens here, it's so lovely and peaceful'. He and his wife have been there for six and half years. As well as operating the lock and the boats – both motor-boats and long-boats – up and down the Thames, there is also, quite near, a rushing, gushing weir which Derek has to watch carefully, as it is with this that he can control the water which comes through the lock. I noticed on some tall trees there were rather queer-looking bird boxes fixed. These I found out were for bats. Apparently, a group of people are studying a colony of bats which they hope will settle and make their home at Shifford lock, but I couldn't find out any further details.

On my way back from the lock, I noticed an old willow tree from which at some time a large branch had almost broken off. This was lying flat on the ground, but there was still life there and lovely tall young branches had grown from that horizontal one – it was quite an unusual sight.

My last two ports of call in this June chapter were Chimney and Old Shifford, and still, at the tail end of the month, the hot sun bore down.

First I called on Miss P. Gauntlett who lives in the farmhouse at Chimney. The hamlet of Chimney consists of one farmhouse, two farm cottages and another house which Miss Gauntlett's farm foreman lives in. It all belongs to Miss Gauntlett who is the fifth generation of farmers to have lived there. She told me that the old name for Chimney was 'Chemengne', which she understood means 'The way through the ford', and that several skeletons have been uncovered in some of her fields, where a number of excavations have been carried out over the years. The finds have proved to be part of an

The delightful Shifford lock

Anglo-Saxon cemetery. It is strange that quite a few of the remote places that I have been to along the Thames seem to have been – many many years ago – much bigger places than they are now. I wonder why there was a decline in the numbers of people? Some say that it was the period of the Black Death.

The next village along the Thames is Old Shifford – another fairly small place consisting of one farmhouse, two cottages, a bungalow and a church. But when I was talking to Mrs Carter who owns the Manor Farm there, she agreed that Old Shifford was, years ago, much bigger, and in King Alfred's

day it was a very important place. According
to the leaflet about the church of St Mary's,
'Shifford was virtually the first Parliamentary
meeting-place in this country, for it was here that
Alfred the Great called together in 890 his Wise
Men and his Royal Court, to attend what has
been called the "Mother of all Parliaments".'

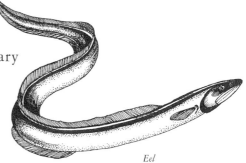

Eel

Today Shifford is a delightfully quiet place with
the river flowing a field away from Mrs Carter's home, where a huge herd of
inquisitive cows came to see what two females were doing strolling in their
field.

'Have you seen anything like this?' Mrs Carter asked me later as we went
to enter a small open porch at the rear of the house. I could see by the mess
on the floor that she was referring to swallows. And there, on a beam just
next to a nest were six small heads, all in a row. The babies were too big to
fit into the nest and, she said, they were not quite old enough to fly. They
certainly made a lovely picture and were not the least disturbed by us
walking underneath the beam. Mrs Carter said that every year there is
always a swallow's nest in the porch, but six youngsters is the most she has
ever seen.

For the first two weeks of July, the hot sun bore down – some days it was apparently hotter in Great Britain than in Barbados. And the spring-sown corn in the fields around my home was definitely 'on the turn', as my old gramp used to say when the spring-sown barley changed from fawn to golden brown – while ribbons of brilliant scarlet poppies wove in and out of the winter-sown crops, which were ripe and ready to cut. In meadows, on common land and on grass verges, masses of wild flowers bloomed: yellow ragwort, purple knapweed, pale blue scabious, golden ladies bedstraw and daisy-like feverfew, while great clumps of rose bay willow herb, sometimes called 'fire of the woods', grew profusely – mostly on waste land – and the white bell-shaped flowers of the giant bindweed climbed and bloomed over the hedgerows.

Today I was making for Newbridge, and later the village and lock at Northmoor – my next rendezvous with the Thames.

About a mile before I reached my first port of call, there was a hold-up while a farmer, his wife and a couple of sleek sheep dogs moved a huge flock of sheep from one field to another – about 300 yards away on the other side of the road. The woman was standing guard by the gate where the sheep were to go in, making sure that they didn't go any further. At the back the farmer, who spoke very quietly to his dogs, was manoeuvring the flock along. I stopped and shut off the engine. I was in no hurry on this beautiful summer day. Just where I pulled up an elderly man was leaning heavily on a gate, watching the proceedings.

'What a lovely picture that makes', I remarked.

CHAPTER SEVEN

The Woods be Blue

High Summer

A flash of red
Vibrant and beautiful
Flames across the hillside
Streaming through the green wheat
Like a bright ribbon
The scarlet Poppy
Flaunting her summer dress
Like a gaudy woman
Stirring our hearts
Outwitting the gentle Rose
Firing our blood
With pent-up emotion
Searing our limbs
With the desires of youth.

Mollie Harris

Poppy, the flower of remembrance

'Ah! that it do', he replied. 'I minds the times when I was shepherd in these parts – ah, fer nigh on fifty years', he went on, 'But I be got that rheumaticky bein' out in all winds and weathers fer all that time, I can only just manage to walk this far from home', nodding in the direction of a cottage a few yards back down the road.

'But I do so love to see 'um still – some folk sez "as silly as a ship" [sheep] but they byent be silly. My flock knowed every word I said to 'um.'

By now the young farmer had got his flock safely in the field, and he and his wife and the dogs came walking

---

A field of glorious poppies

along the road towards us and the farmhouse.

'Don't take too much notice of what old Fred says', the farmer said to me, laughing. Then he went on speaking to Fred, 'No, you know I don't mean that, don't you, Fred?'

He went on, addressing me, 'Best shepherd for miles around, both my gramp and my father always said "wish I'd got a fellow like him working for me". But they don't breed 'em like him nowadays.'

And they passed by, a couple of very healthy looking, friendly people.

'Do you think this weather's going to hold?' I asked Fred.

He cocked a watery eye towards a wooded area, well over three miles away as the crow flies, and said, 'Ah, tha's going to be fine for a few more days yet, see, the woods be blue', he said, pointing to a mass of trees in the distance, 'Tha's a sure sign of settled weather.'

I looked in the direction that Fred was pointing – the woods did have a bluey-grey look, not mist, but a sort of blue blur over the trees, as the hot sun bore down on them.

'Well, it's time I got on my way', I said, as I called cheerio to the old fellow, 'Hope to see you again one day.'

'Ah, I hopes so, too', he replied. 'That bin nice to 'ave a chat with somebody who got time to stop and listen.'

I reached Newbridge which, despite its name, is in fact one of the oldest over the Thames, but Radcot – further up the Thames and which we have already visited – is about fifty years older. Both places were scenes of battles; at Newbridge, during the Civil War, Cromwell's men captured the bridge in May 1644, causing King Charles I to retreat northwards. Here is an extract from a poem on the Thames, written by John William Pitt:

The second oldest bridge on the Thames at Newbridge

This bridge has great antiquity, and thus belies its name
For, like historic Radcot bridge, it owes its present fame,
To having been the scene of stormy battle long ago.
When Charles 1st was England's King – and Parliament his foe.

I parked the car and went in to The Rose Revived – a delightful river-side hotel and restaurant, nowadays quite sophisticated – a great difference to the fairly ordinary pub that it was in the days of my youth. It was here that my sisters and I used to come swimming on summer Sunday mornings. We would cycle from Ducklington, although we already had our own river – the Windrush – almost outside our door in which we and all the locals swam and the cows wandered across the 'shallows'. At Newbridge, however, there were lots of fellows to flirt with, young undergrads from Oxford – that in itself was worth the ride from Ducklington!

Mine host at The Rose Revived was very busy that morning, organizing lunch for many folk who were either sitting outside by the river or waiting in the cool restaurant, so there was little time to talk. A huge board on the wall of one of the rooms told of the history of the place. It appears that at one time The Rose – as it was known for years – once belonged to Northmoor Manor, which was then owned by the Harcourts. In 1851 there was a very busy wharf there which was sold around that time to William Marriott, coal merchant of Witney. To this day there is still a firm of Marriott coal merchants operating at nearby Witney. In William Marriott's time, coal and salt came down from the Midlands – first by canal, and then by river, for distribution in the Oxfordshire and Berkshire areas. Stone was brought on barges via the River Windrush which flows into the Thames at Newbridge, from Taynton Quarry near Burford, which at that time belonged to Thomas Strong, one of Wren's master builders. Thomas Strong supplied excellent quality stone for building bridges over the Thames, for Windsor Castle, the Oxford colleges and also to help rebuild the City of London after the Great Fire. River transport

The Maybush at Newbridge

at that time was excellent while most roads were in a disastrous condition.

There is no wharf there now, but it is a delightful river-side area that attracts a great number of people, as well as motor cruisers and other boats of all description which stop there on their way up river to the stripling Thames.

I crossed over the beautiful bridge and wandered into the other pub — The Maybush. This river-side tavern really seems part of the bridge itself, with a wonderful atmosphere all of its own — warm, comfortable and low ceilinged, where the traveller can get hot or cold meals seven days a week, and there is a marvellous view of the river and green meadows beyond. Here, too, there is a huge caravan park where fishermen and their families enjoy the beautiful surroundings. Julie Cockburn, landlady of the Maybush, was also busy with lunches.

The Rose Revived

'It's cook's day off', she explained.

The young man serving in the bar did tell me that the old 'uns had told him that, years ago, when The Maybush was in Berkshire, they were allowed to keep open a half an hour longer than The Rose Revived and that, as soon as that one closed, the old fellows would leg it over the bridge and enjoy another half hour's drinking time at The Maybush. Both now are in Oxfordshire.

Of course July is probably the peak time for river trade, with several holiday-makers popping in for drinks and meals, and it was a case of 'gather ye rosebuds while ye may', so I took my leave, and made for the nearby village of Northmoor. Here, again, the roadsides were lush with wild summer flowers and the trees heavy-leafed and dark green. But where was Northmoor lock? I'd never seen a signpost to it, although I've lived around this area for many years. So I knocked at the door of a house and asked the owner how to get to the lock – wherever it was!

'Go a few yards along this road and turn left. You then drive down a lane for quite a long way, then park the car and walk over a couple of fields and you'll come to it. There is another way to get to it, but you have to go to Appleton village – which is rather a long way round from here. Yes, your best bet is down the lane', she said.

Thanking her kindly, I set off, following her instructions, and eventually I came to Northmoor lock, where the lock-keeper, Colin Buddin, was busy letting a boat through. In gaps in his very busy afternoon we chattered. He has been there twenty-two years and, of course, knows the Thames thereabouts like the back of his hand. He told me that thirty years ago there was only a footpath to the lock and that one day a man broke his ankle there. Help was such a long time getting to him that complications set in and he died. After that tragedy, a road from Appleton was built. At one time there were osier beds nearby where willows were grown, not just for basket making as many were, but also for making covers for wine bottles. Throughout the years Colin has been working there he has found out much about the Thames, and tells the story of a man called Leon Weal, who years ago was the lock-keeper at Rushy lock. To earn a bit of extra cash he used to catch eels there and take them into the nearby town of Faringdon to sell. One night, however, he had had such a good catch of eels that he couldn't take them out of their cage traps fast enough – on that memorable night he caught 180 pounds of eels!

Another happening – but this time more recent – was that his son (who incidentally is now his assistant), a keen fisherman, kept losing his fishing tackle at one particular spot because it would get caught up in something in this hole in the river, where quite a lot of fish congregated. So Colin thought he'd try and find the cause. With grappling irons he first pulled out a huge piece of wood; next time it was a great lump of old iron; and on the third try, up came a huge fender, the sort that folk have around their fires. It was

Lonely Northmoor lock

this that had been the cause of the trouble. Anyhow, in time Colin cleaned up this solid brass fender.

'And I've still got it', he told me. 'Shiny and lovely in me front room.'

Of course, the Thames is now controlled by the Thames Conservancy, but that has not always been the case and years ago land and weir owners used to charge a lot for boats to go through. One day Colin was in Oxford Museum finding out what he could about the river, and he came across an old receipt where one boat owner, in 1860, had had to pay the sum of £45 for his loaded boat to go through a lock situated between Oxford and Burcot.

All this time – on this lovely summer's day – Colin and his son were busy letting boats through; a good life in the fresh air and sunshine, but a hard one – but Colin wouldn't change it for anything!

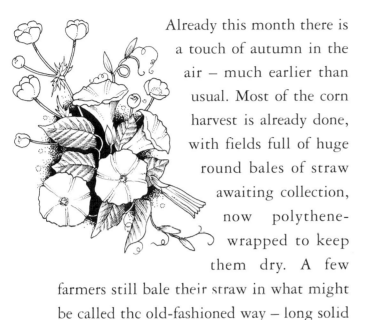

Already this month there is a touch of autumn in the air – much earlier than usual. Most of the corn harvest is already done, with fields full of huge round bales of straw awaiting collection, now polythene-wrapped to keep them dry. A few farmers still bale their straw in what might be called the old-fashioned way – long solid bales, but at least they can be built into ricks, something which is impossible to do with those big round ones. Now great flocks of starlings search the stubble for grubs. Some farmers have already got on with the ploughing, with hundreds of gulls following the five- or six-furrowed plough which can cover the ground very quickly. A field these days can be soon cleared, and some are already planted in no time. In fact I saw one with a soft green sheen where the newly sown corn was coming through.

Tall, purple loosestrife was growing in masses along the damp river-side, and I saw one very big clump of yellow loosestrife – not a very common sight in this part of the countryside. Giant bindweed climbed over the hedges and the smaller lesser plant, which is white with pinky-mauve stripes – like little girls dresses – grew on the verge side along with clumps of white-topped thistle, now gone to seed. In the fields I saw quite a lot of baby rabbits, but not many pheasants or partridge.

I reached Bablockhythe. It was here that the poet, Matthew Arnold, wrote the immortal words in the poem called 'The Scholar Gypsy': 'crossing the stripling Thames at Bablockhythe, trailing in the cool stream thy fingers wet'.

Summer's End

Sea-filled fields of yellow
Sweet smelling mallow
Winds its way down turning lanes
In the bubbled heat
And a bee buzzes by
The trees in the haze
Poppies dance as the train goes past
At high speed
In the afternoon
With the lark wearing his summer cloak
The tower swims on the horizon vising
Rising with the swallows
Taking the summer with them.

Gary Woodley

The poem, a long one, is about a young Oxford undergraduate who left his studies and roamed about all his life with gypsies to learn their ways.

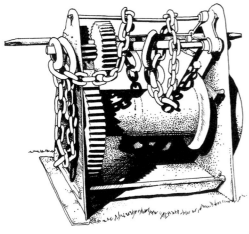

The remains of the ferry

When I was young, 'Bab' – as it was called locally – was a quiet river crossing with a very large flat wooden ferry-boat which carried cars, farm vehicles and passengers backwards and forwards. It was the only way at that point to cross over from the Oxfordshire side into Berkshire, to reach Cumnor village and beyond. There has been a ferry of some sort there for at least six hundred years. I remember riding across the river on it. I can't remember how much the ride cost, probably a penny.

There were only about six people on the wooden barge-like contraption, and I thought that a man operated the ferry by levering it across with a paddle attached to the chain. But if the ferry was loaded up with heavier things, then I *think* that a man worked it by turning a huge handle which was connected to heavy chains fixed from one side of the river bank to the other. Today the old ferry is no more; apparently it was smashed in a very bad storm some years ago, although you can still see part of the equipment outside the pub – the Ferryman Inn. When boats came along, the chains which stretched across the river were in some way lowered on to the river bed so that they could pass through. Mind you, that was long ago, so I hope my memories are correct! Of course, there has been an inn there for centuries – in my young days it was called The Chequers – but in fairly recent times it closed for about five years. Then it was bought by a young man called Peter Kellard. Now it has been completely refurbished, but keeping many of the old interesting features. Peter told me that there is now comfortable accommodation there, and they serve a wonderful variety of meals to residents and to passing boat people and travellers. Today, if anyone wishes to cross over to 't'other side' of the river, they are taken across in a small boat powered by an outboard motor. The owner of the inn is trying to get a proper ferry crossing for vehicles – but so far without success.

Nearby is a huge caravan park, with permanent homes for many folk. There is also a separate holiday caravan park with up-to-date facilities and, of course, all adjacent to the River Thames.

I moved on to the lovely village of Stanton Harcourt, not directly alongside the river but not far from it. There has been a village there at least since Saxon times – then called 'Stan-tun' or Stone town (a settlement near the stones) because, until 1940, three huge Neolithic stones called 'The Devil's Quoits' stood there. These stones – so one picturesque story tells us – were cast there by the devil when he was

The river near Chequers, Bablockhythe

Upstream from Bablockhythe (old and new)

The lovely gardens at Stanton Harcourt

playing quoits on nearby Beacon Hill. But historians tell us that the
stones were, in fact, part of a great megalithic circle which the experts say
was nine hundred yards in diameter. I can remember seeing those three
great stones many years ago, but they were buried when an aerodrome
was built there in the early part of the last war. When contractors started
digging the huge gravel pits at Stanton Harcourt and the nearby villages,
it was hoped that maybe they would discover The Devil's Quoits, but so
far no luck! But much HAS been found over the years from the millions of
tons of gravel extraction, including stone tools, hand axes and remains of
mammoths. Just recently a 200,000-year-old, 3-metre long mammoth

tusk was found in a gravel pit which had been left empty, close to the Thames. Many of the other pits have been filled in with thousands of tons of refuse. Eventually some of these will have soil spread over them and crops will again flourish. Others will remain as great lakes where wildlife live, and some have been made into water parks for sailing and water-skiing.

But despite the great area of gravel pits, which are still being worked, the village of Stanton Harcourt remains a lovely spot. The word

The old fireplace in the kitchen at Stanton Harcourt

Harcourt was added to Stanton when the famous Harcourt family first settled there in the early twelfth century. In the fifteenth century they built a magnificent manor house where they would receive visits from the royal family. Now, to see the great medieval kitchen with its blackened walls and its conical roof, and the huge fireplace where an ox could be roasted whole, the great ovens and no chimney – but an ingenious arrangement of shutters in the roof which could be opened to let the smoke out, according to which way the wind was blowing – tells us of the scale on which the Harcourts entertained in those early days. Nearby is a tall tower, the same age as the kitchen, called Pope's Tower, because in a tiny room at the

The old wall ovens in the kitchen at Stanton Harcourt

top of this building Alexander Pope worked on the translation of the fifth volume of Homer's *Iliad*. When it was finished, Pope scratched on a pane of red glass in the window:

> In the year 1718, I, Alexander Pope, finished here the fifth
> volume of Homer.

This pane of glass was removed several years ago, and is now in the possession of the Hon. Mrs Ann Gascoigne, daughter of the late Lord Harcourt, who now resides at the manor house in Stanton Harcourt. Not, of course, the huge place that it was in the fifteenth century, but nevertheless it is still very beautiful, with lovely gardens and lakes which are sometimes open to the public. In the grounds are some of the huge lovely stone-built barns that would have housed the harvest many years ago. There is also a private domestic chapel on the ground floor of Pope's Tower, with a beautiful fan-vaulted stone roof, and a red velvet armchair which was the throne of the Most Revd and the Hon. Edward Vernon Harcourt, Archbishop of York, 1807–47. In the village are the remains of the old stocks, several lovely old thatched cottages, and an inn called the Harcourt Arms which serves delectable meals.

The church of St Michael's, which stands very near to the manor house, is certainly worth a visit to see the ornate Harcourt tombs of the last nine hundred years: Knights of the Garter, Field Marshals, Earls, Ambassadors and even a Lord Chancellor of England and, of course, some of the ladies of that period, too, all dressed in the costumes of the day. Some of these are in the Harcourt Chapel, where

Inscription by Alexandra Pope after completing the fifth volume of Homer's Iliad

Pope's Tower at Stanton Harcourt

The old kitchen at Stanton Harcourt

you can also see the tattered silk standard that Sir Robert Harcourt bore in the Battle of Bosworth. Inside the church are some lovely eighteenth-century oak pews. Outside on the church wall is a memorial to two lovers who, along with many villagers on 31 July 1718, were working in a corn field when a sudden thunderstorm broke. The lightning killed these two sweethearts as they were sheltering in a corn stack – they were John Hewett and Sarah Drew, 'an industrious young man and a virtuous maiden of the parish'. This must have been a terrible tragedy to the villagers.

The old stocks at Stanton Harcourt

Young swifts

On the Thames, between Bablockhythe and Pinkhill lock, there is a place that the locals still call 'Skinner's Bridge' – although the bridge itself disappeared years ago when some over-enthusiastic Oxford undergraduates burned it down. But Henry Taunt – the Victorian writer and photographer who travelled from the Thames head at Trewsbury Mead to London and who also published books about other journeys that he made on the river during the latter part of the nineteenth century – wrote of Joe Skinner, the last landlord there, in his book *A New Map of the River Thames*:

This is one of the new gallows bridges which have taken the place of the old weirs. The old weir, with its couple of quaint thatched cottages, was one of those picturesque places that artists love. It had been in the possession of the Skinners from father to son for a long number of years. It was a little inn, and the last landlord, Joe Skinner, was one of the best hearted, quaintest fellows that ever lived He was original in the highest degree, and it was a rich treat to spend an evening with him and listen to his talk of havoc wrought among the wild ducks, with his stalking horse and tremendous duck gun, or his curious remarks on someone who had been there, and, not understanding him, had rubbed old Joe the wrong way of the wool, getting perhaps a rough setting down. This is all swept away by the march of improvement:

A kestrel hovering for food

the old cottages, the tumbledown weir, and old Joe are all gone, and the place entirely lone and deserted.

Now all that is left are a few wooden stakes at the river's edge, but many older local people still remember the bridge being there. Mr Robert Willis, who in the 1930s lived and worked at Pinkhill Farm with his parents and brothers, but who now lives in Canada, wrote and told me what he remembered of Skinner's Bridge: 'We just thought that it was a link between the residents of Farmoor and Stanton Harcourt. The residents of Farmoor had no pub of their own, so on fine summer evenings many of them would wend their way over the bridge, via the footpath, to the Harcourt Arms at Stanton Harcourt, and savour the delights that *mine host* had to offer. The bridge was also used by many fishermen, and it was rumoured that somewhere there, there was a body of water connected with the river which formed a rush-covered pond and contained pike and of tremendous proportions – only seen, but never caught!'

And so it was on to Pinkhill lock. Along the river-side, bushes were dripping with hips and haws and the air was filled with dozens and dozens of craneflies (daddylonglegs), and grey and pied wagtails strutted in the pale sunshine.

Tim Brown, the present lock-keeper, a slim, very fit-looking young man, has been there since 1980. I asked him if turning those huge wheels and pushing the heavy lock gates open and shut to let the boats through was very hard work.

'Let's say you get used to it', he replied, good humouredly. 'But most lock-keepers at sometime or other suffer either from "lock-keeper's back" or double hernia. Of course', he added, 'rumour has it that one day all this gate opening will be done by the push of a button; apparently', he went on, 'some have already changed to automation.'

It was a mild autumn day and there were still a few motor-boats coming through. Tim admitted that not so many folk were using the river as they did way back in the '70s and early '80s. 'It's the package holidays, you see. I'm afraid we can't guarantee hot sunshine all the while. In fact', he added, 'this September has been the wettest for many years.'

Lock-keeper's house at Pinkhall

As we were chatting I noticed some funny sort of metal frames attached to the electric wires above us, where the great pylons marched across the land. I asked what they were.

'Ah!', said Tim, 'they have saved many a swan's life. Before those wire frames were fixed, the swans – who use this stretch to land and take off, because of the nearness of the river – used to fly straight into the wires and many died. Then someone came up with this idea, which is brilliant.'

Just across the way, in a field almost joining on to the lock, is a pump-house which pumps water into the great nearby reservoir of Farmoor. The first phase of this was built in 1967 and the present one – the second phase – in 1977; 40,000 gallons of water a day is taken out of the Thames to keep the reservoir full.

There is a huge meadow nearby where, before the last war, the famous woman aviator, Amy Johnson, used to come with her plane and practise taking off and landing. Later, during the war, the farmer who rented the field, a Mr Franklin, almost covered the meadow with old farm machinery and broken-down cars to stop the Germans landing on it – a precaution if we had been invaded! Now, the meadow is called 'Pinkhill Meadow Nature Reserve', opened a while ago by TV naturalist Julian Pettifer, and recounted in the current *Thames* magazine:

Grey wagtail

One of the most successful projects so far has been the creation of the Pinkhill Meadow Nature Reserve at Farmoor. Opened by TV naturalist Julian Pettifer the reserve was the result of a successful three-year partnership with the NRA. Four hectares of meadow between the River Thames and Farmoor Reservoir were carefully excavated by removing 20,000 cubic metres of earth. Work was carried out in three phases with Thames and the NRA jointly contributing a total of £180,000 over three years. The nature reserve was designed to promote wetland nature conservation and includes a rich variety of habitats, including shallow pools, wet meadow, reed beds and a pond with gravel islands. A colourful array of bird-life includes Curlew, Hobby, Lapwing, Redshank and the Tufted Duck. This spring two pairs of the rare Little Ringed Plover reared five chicks. Now well established, Pinkhill has become a firm favourite with visitors. Schoolchildren are welcomed and on organised trips Thames supplies them with education packs containing information, pictures and posters. 'Pinkhill has also been a great success with birdwatchers

Hobby, the smallest bird of prey

who have told us that it is the best spot in Oxfordshire', said Conservation Manager Mike Crafer.

I understand that a wonderful assortment of wild flowers are growing in the meadow too.

Pinkhill lock has had several lock-keepers over the years, but one notable one was Mr Henry Smith who lived here with his family from 1908 to 1939. Mr Smith, as well as being an excellent lock-keeper, was also a wonderful gardener and for several years won the first prize of £2 for the best-kept garden between Osney lock, Oxford, to St John's lock at Lechlade. Unfortunately there are no such competitions like that these days!

In the early days the Smith family lived in a wooden and asbestos bungalow, but later on moved into the lovely stone house – which still stands today. Mr Smith's two remaining children, Mrs Iris Harris and Mr Ken Smith, told me what the conditions were like when they lived there and how – when the floods were up – their father used to row them over to Swinford Bridge so that they could then walk up to Eynsham to school.

'We was all very happy and content there', Mrs Harris told me. 'There was plenty of things to interest us: we could spend all day in the fields in summer, playing games in the hay, swinging on the willow tree branches, picking the lovely wild flowers that grew there, and swimming in a place we called "the shallows". Our dad fixed us up a swing in the garden and a see-saw, and we was never bored.' Ken Smith said that in the summer lots of youngsters from Wales used to come and camp in the big meadow. These were children of miners who were out of work. It was a lovely change for them to be out in the fresh air and cooking their food on camp fires. It was properly organized, of course, with grown-ups looking after them.

My next call was at Eynsham lock, about a mile from Pinkhill, where I met Mr McCreadie who has been lock-keeper there for twenty-four years. As we chatted by the river-side, dozens of fish – chub and dace, some weighing two to three pounds I should think – swam about in the deep dark river. Mr McCreadie told me how things had altered considerably at Eynsham lock over the years. The present lock and house was built in 1928 – before then there was a flash weir, also known as a paddle and rymer weir. The nearby wharf stream, now rather overgrown with reeds and weeds, was used when heavy goods

A circle of posts where paddles and rymers were kept

were brought up by river to Eynsham. But the remains of a huge tree trunk can still be seen; this was on a swivel which could be swung across the stream. Also nearby is a ring of posts enclosed in iron where the paddles and rymers were kept locked. When the water had to be held back these paddles and rymers were forced into a huge sill at the bed of the stream, so it was the tree trunk, rymers and paddles that held the water back. Today there is a bridge for walkers to cross, but I was intrigued by this great old rotting tree trunk.

'Is it oak?' I asked him.

'No', he replied, with an Irish lilt in his voice, 'I think it's ellum.'

I smiled to myself, I hadn't heard elm pronounced like that for years.

Just a few yards away from Eynsham lock is Swinford Toll Bridge, with its elegant stone span over the river, which wheeled vehicles have to pay to cross – much to the disgust of the motorists. It was in 1769 when King George III's coach nearly came to grief there because the river was in flood and the ford under deep water, that he decreed that the owner – the 4th Earl of Abingdon – should build a bridge over the Thames there and charge a toll for everything crossing over it; the monies collected would be tax-free *for ever*. Now only mechanized vehicles have to pay, but at one time owners of animals, cyclists – and in the early days, I believe, even pedestrians had to pay. The old board from it showing some of the charges is now in Woodstock Museum:

SWINFORD BRIDGE TOLL GATE

By an Act of the 7th of King George the 3rd
The following Tolls are to be paid at this Gate for every time of
  passing

	pence
For every Carriage whatsoever with 4 Wheels	4
With less than 4 Wheels	2

Lock-keeper's house at Swinford

For every Horse, Gelding, Mare, Mule or Ass,
Laden or not laden, drawing or not drawing. } 1
For every Ox, Bull, Cow, Steer or Heifer, } ½
For every Calf, Swine, Sheep or Lamb. } ¼

J.D. Percy
Manager

Swinford Toll Bridge

And so to my village of Eynsham, about a mile from Swinford Toll Bridge, where I have lived for the past forty-odd years. A pleasant place, with the charming old square surrounded by stone cottages, and the elegant church of St Leonard's dominating the area. The church is dedicated to St Leonard, the patron saint of prisoners. Nothing really remains of the huge Benedictine abbey which, until the Dissolution of the Monasteries, was the second wealthiest in the land. Several of the old cottages, including mine, have carved stones built into them. It is believed that after the abbey fell into ruin, the locals used the stone to

Eynsham church and square

build their own cottages, many of them dating from the early eighteenth century. These days Eynsham is a go-ahead place with several new estates (both private and council) built around as well as a number of small modern factories on the outskirts employing a number of local people; with good street lighting, fine schools and modern shops, a good community spirit abounds.

One man who is Eynsham born and bred is Ron May, who worked on the Thames for thirty-two years. His father and grandfather before him, too, worked almost all their lives on the river. His father, for some reason, was known as Soldier May and Ron always as Young Soldier. At one time Ron was dredger-master and drove a one hundred ton steam dredger, which had to be towed up and down the river by a great tug. The dredger dug up all sorts of things, including glazed tiles, Roman axe heads, a 2,000-year-old sword, lemonade bottles with glass marbles in and once, at Lechlade, a skull. This caused great excitement and the police were informed who thought, at the time, that it might have been the result of a fairly recent tragedy – but after examination it was found to be thousands of years old. It was Ron's gang who brought the huge figure of Old Father Thames from the source at Trewsbury Mead to its present home at Lechlade. One of their lorries had previously collected it from the Crystal Palace Exhibition and had taken it to Trewsbury Mead years before.

Ron and I chatted for a while about the Thames and I spoke of the Inglesham round-house near Lechlade.

'Ah', he said, 'there used to be quite a few of them along the canals', and he went on, 'You knows why they built 'um round, don't you?'

'No, I don't', I said, leaning forward – here, I thought, was a bit of local history that I could write about.

'Well', he said with a grin, 'they built 'um round so that the cats couldn't s—— in the corners. Well! that's what all the Thames fellows says, anyway', and he threw back his head and laughed a good hearty laugh.

Well, Ron finished up as an area supervisor for the Thames area, but has now retired from the Thames Conservancy.

Cat (watch the corners)

Young fox cub

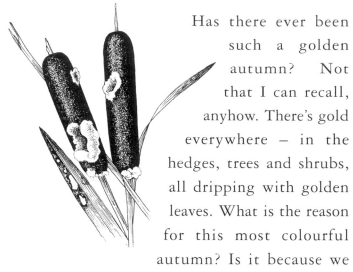

Has there ever been such a golden autumn? Not that I can recall, anyhow. There's gold everywhere – in the hedges, trees and shrubs, all dripping with golden leaves. What is the reason for this most colourful autumn? Is it because we had four or five very sharp frosts, along with days of brilliant sunshine, around the second week of this month? Whatever the reason for this phenomenal and colourful autumn, it is being enjoyed and remarked about by many people.

CHAPTER TEN

Golden Glory

OCTOBER

Well, on my next wander along the Thames, I left Eynsham lock and walked towards Kings weir, my next port of call. After leaving Eynsham behind, the Thames sweeps along the edge of the beautiful Wytham Woods for quite a few miles. The wood, some six hundred acres of it, looked magnificent in the autumn sunshine which seemed to bring out the colours of the many different trees more vividly – oak, ash, lime, sycamore and many many others – their autumn tints ranging from pale yellow and brilliant gold, to amber and russet red, and on to the deep maroon red of the elder trees. There were several spindle bushes dotted about, their shocking pink berries with the bright orange middles showed up on the leafless branches. And the hazel trees, also leafless, but with minute new catkins on were a promise of spring already. Someone in the wood was doing some clearing up and there was a pleasant smell of a leafy bonfire as the smoke wafted across my pathway, a pathway which had

End of Autumn

Bedecked in jewelled cobwebs,

The gentle branches

of the silver Birch,

Shine through the morning mist,

Then, loosening their hold

The golden leaves

Drift to the ground

Spilling over the dew-wet grass,

Like coins from a miser's hoard.

Mollie Harris

The Thames looking onto Wytham Wood

actually disappeared under a yellow, golden and russet speckled carpet of leaves. I scuffed through them – who can resist doing this in autumn? Some of the leaves had blown into the river, looking like little coloured ships as the deep dark water carried them downstream. The wood, which for centuries was owned by the earls of Abingdon, later belonged for many years to Colonel ffennell who, in the early forties, gave the entire wood to the University of Oxford. A deed was set up which provided that 'Every care should be taken to preserve the woods in their present state of natural beauty', and that 'The University will take all reasonable steps to preserve and maintain the woodlands and will use them for the instruction of suitable students, and will provide facilities for research.' Permits are issued to walk in the woods, but in the interest of research it is necessary to restrict the number issued.

Then Cassington church spire loomed up out of the now misty river-side, and soon I reached the spot where the beautiful River Evenlode slips into the Thames.

Near here I left the river, and drove on a few miles till I came to a sign to a private road leading to Kings lock. I left the main road and walked along the river-side road to the lock, where I saw lots of Canada geese, mallard, moorhens and the flash of a beautiful kingfisher – which brightened a rather dull morning. And here I met the very cheerful amiable lock-keeper, Leigh Fenton, who has been at Kings for the last eighteen years. The gardens surrounding the lock looked particularly colourful and tidy, and the beech hedges shielding the shrubs were newly cut – ready for winter, so Leigh told me. Kings weir, or Kings lock, has nothing to do with royalty, he said. It's from an Anglo-Saxon word 'Kinisesweir', meaning something to do with cattle and pigs which evidently roamed the countryside in great numbers in that area. There has been a lock of one sort or another there since Roman times, when it was called a pound lock. In 1189 it was used mostly for catching fish for the vergers of Wolvercote, but in 1863 it was a flash lock with double-paddle gates.

Then in 1928 the Thames Conservancy built the present lock along with a lovely stone house. For several years, Leigh told me, there was no roadway to the lock – just a muddy path. So, if they needed shopping they travelled by boat, and, once, Leigh's wife Janet put in a request to the Conservancy to keep a donkey to enable her to take the children on it as far as the main road so that they could catch the school bus. Before this, however, in 1977, when the house and lock were surrounded by deep flood water and Leigh's wife was expecting a baby, the ambulance couldn't get through – there was no road anyway, apart from the floods – so Mrs Fenton and a friend struggled on foot across Pixie Mead, where they eventually reached the road and the ambulance that whisked her off to hospital. Tragically, it was too late, and Mrs Fenton lost her baby.

After years of asking for a roadway and with local dignitaries also pressing for it, the present mile-long road was built alongside the river.

All along my Thames journey, I had been making enquiries from the various river men as to where the River Isis began and where the Thames continued again – Oxford folk are always referring to the river as the Isis.

'Ah', Leigh told me, 'It's all the Thames really. It was some Oxford dons many years ago who named the Oxford area of the Thames, the Isis. It's taken from the old Roman name for the river – Thames, Thamesis or Tamesis – but, as I say, it's all the Thames really.'

'It's wonderfully quiet here', I remarked.

'Ah, it's not always so, we've had our excitement here before now – apart from the 13,000 boats that pass through here in a year, once in 1985 we caught a couple of prisoners who had escaped from Oxford Prison! Oh, yes, we had really got them under control before the police arrived!'

I could have stayed and listened to Leigh all day, but both he and I had work to do, so I back-pedalled a bit and came to the delightful village of Wytham, not directly alongside the Thames but very near. The whole village, apart from the inn and the church and, I think, the old rectory on

Wytham Woods skirting the Thames

Autumn tints and a lovely old bridge

whose grounds two modern dwelling houses have been built, belongs to the University of Oxford. It is beautifully maintained and attracts many visitors with its old world charm.

I remember an elderly lady, who lived near me in Eynsham a few years back, had told me that she had an old uncle and aunt who lived at Wytham. When she was about eight years old, she, her mother, father, four brothers and two sisters used to walk from Eynsham, through the woods and 'over the top' of quite a steep hill, and then down to their little cottage, which was up a lane somewhere just outside the village of Wytham. Twice a year they went visiting the old uncle and aunt there, and she told me that for dinner they always had boiled bacon, taters and swede mashed together, and brussel sprouts, followed by a giant spotted-dick boiled pudding which her aunt doled out in thick chunks and covered with runny custard – oh it was lovely! The pudding and the bacon were cooked in the same big black saucepan over the fire, and the liquid that they were boiled in went to mix up the pig food – nothing was wasted in those days.

'My goodness', she said, 'didn't that dinner go down good. We was starving hungry, 'cos we'd walked miles and miles from Eynsham.' And she went on, 'Mind you, there was always a bit of a job cutting up the big piece of bacon. It had to be big to feed us lot. One year, I remember my aunt was grumbling about not having a sharp knife, when my uncle said, "stop yer moanin', Mabel, give it us yer. I'll soon get that apart". And he took it out to his old shed, sat this great lump of hot bacon on an old chopping block, and set about chopping the meat up with a small axe that he used to chop the fire lighting wood with! And there were bits of fat bacon flying about all over the place. I've often laughed over that, folks don't do things like that nowadays, do they?'

And she went on reminiscing.

'I remember the long walk back home through Wytham Woods. It was autumn time with lots of leaves fluttering down, and we children tried to catch them, and there were red squirrels running up and down the trees, too. I started crying 'cos my legs were tired and they hurt, so my dad hoisted me up on his shoulders and carried me the rest of the way home.'

I left the lovely quiet village of Wytham and made my way up the road to Godstow and the famous Trout Inn, which was originally built in 1133 as a

Tool used for chopping the bacon

The famous Trout Inn at Godstow

hospice for visitors to Godstow nunnery. Much later it became the Trout Inn, which is a very popular rendezvous for Oxford undergraduates, and in summer thousands of folk visit this lovely old river-side inn to dine, or to sit on the terrace, while elegant peacocks strut around them, and gaze at the river splashing over the weir, while hundreds of trout thrash about in the foamy water. There used to be an elegant wooden bridge which spanned the river, over which people could walk to have their drinks on the other side in a sort of island paradise with shady trees and stone ornaments including a huge stone lion. The remains of the bridge can still be seen and the garden is

beautifully maintained, but visitors
are no longer allowed in there. A
locked wrought-iron gate leading
to it from the roadway is decorated
with ornate crowns and there are
English roses on it, too – but I
couldn't find out what connection they
had with the inn.

Stone lion in the secret garden at Godstow

So I walked along the river-side to what
remains of the famous Godstow nunnery. There are
still some high stone walls left there, although much of it is in ruins having been

Ruins at Godstow nunnery

GOLDEN GLORY

October

Hedge-sparrow

Great crested grebe

destroyed during the Civil War — it must have been a very large place in its day. Long before that, however, a beautiful young girl called Rosamund de Clifford was a pupil there. One day she was walking with her maidens along the river-side, when King Henry II, who was coming from his palace in Oxford, saw her. She eventually left the nunnery, became the king's mistress, had two sons by him and lived in a mysterious bower in Woodstock. The king would visit her there, following a thin trail of silken cord. The tale goes on to say, that his queen — Eleanor — learned of Rosamund and her hiding place and supposedly poisoned her; but others say that she returned to Godstow nunnery, where she died in 1176 in penitence and seclusion and was buried in a magnificent tomb there.

I left this sad ruin and walked on to nearby Godstow lock. Unfortunately the lock-keeper, Mr Wilson, was far too busy to talk to me, so I wandered on along the river bank, past the lock, where a solitary heron was standing, grey and silent. There was quite a lot of wildlife on the river — a couple of swans, several ducks and a lone crested grebe. Over on the other side of the Thames I could see the vast Port Meadow, which I shall write about in the next chapter. On my way back, a hedge-sparrow — or to use its proper name, a Dunnock — flew into a nearby crab-apple tree, which still had a few coloured fruit hanging on its almost leafless boughs.

The weather had changed dramatically since I had started out, and a delicate mist was beginning to float over the Thames. It was time I made my way towards home and a warm fire.

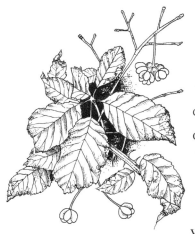

November on the whole is always thought of as a dull, colourless, month. But on my way to Wolvercote, my next port of call on the Thames, things looked very different. There was quite a lot of colour in the hedgerows and fields: the yellow, red and gold branches of the willows, the glossy green ivy and thick-berried holly, the fawny-gold spikes – just before they drop – on the larch branches (the only conifer to lose its leaves in winter), hedges of wine-red haws (the country name for these is 'assies'), the vibrant scarlet-hip berries of the dog rose (were there that many flowers on them in June?) and deep green leafy conifers showing up against the now, lovely bare branches of beech and oak trees. Out in the fields, bright cock-pheasants strutted about proudly, accompanied by their dull-coloured wives, and a few white-tailed rabbits on the headlands were nibbling the fresh green of autumn-planted corn. Some of the fields were newly ploughed, rich and brown, awaiting the winter frosts to break up the clods into a fine tilth ready for the spring planting, while great flocks of peewit, seagulls and starlings wheeled overhead. Yes! there's plenty of colour and things to observe in November – if you care to look!

And so I came to Wolvercote village (where Tolkien lies buried in the churchyard there) and to the papermill that has been there for centuries. Originally it did not produce paper because in the very early years it was a flour mill. Then, in 1643, when King Charles I was in Oxford, he had it converted into a huge forge to make swords for his army. By 1674 it had become a papermill, mostly making fine paper for the Bible presses and for hymnal papers. This is no longer the case today, although with new very modern machinery, computers and know-how, the demand for many other types of paper keeps the Wolvercote mill very busy.

When I first came to live in Eynsham, I was eager to find out why the street in which I live is called Mill Street; yet, there was no sign of a mill. Apparently it had been pulled down years ago, and much of the rubble and stone was used as a road base when the nearby A40 was being built in the early 1930s. But I was intrigued about this lost mill, and during my research I discovered that at one time it had also produced the fine paper for Bible presses, and that it had once belonged to the Swann family (who also lived in my street), who owned – or part-owned – Wolvercote mill. Oxford University Press needed more paper for the Bibles and for the new prayer book which had been authorized in 1662. George Hagar, a London dyer, played the most important part at Eynsham mill. He was granted a patent in 1682 for his improved method of making white paper by sizing the pulp in the mortar. The mill continued to produce paper to the end of the nineteenth century. The reason for the closure of Eynsham mill – at least for paper making – was the fact that, at the turn of the century, much imported paper was coming into the country so the work was transferred to Wolvercote mill, and the Eynsham one became – among other things – a rag, flock and glue mill. All this came to an end during the 1920s, and now there is a thriving trout farm nearby.

By now the fog had come down over the river at Wolvercote and it was time I made my way home.

A preening pintail

A few days later I journeyed to Binsey and Port Meadow.

Binsey is a delightful, small village near Oxford. Clustered around the village green are a few lovely stone cottages and farm buildings, and the 500-year-old Perch Inn – which was largely rebuilt in 1977 after a nasty fire destroyed much of the building. The inn was restored in great detail and originality, so that when you enter you are met by lovely oak beams, flagstone floors and stone hearths, yet it still retains its lovely part-thatched roof. Like lots of old buildings, the Perch is supposed to be haunted. A long time ago, a naval petty officer, who lived nearby, drowned

Binsey village viewed from the river

himself in the river because he was heavily in debt. And it is his ghost that folk say they have sighted – sometimes wandering along the river bank, and sometimes standing at the bar of the Perch. The 'Phantom Sailor' – as he is often called – did not appear on the day that I visited; the meal, however, was excellent.

I made my way up the lane towards the church of St Margaret. There had been a sharp frost overnight and the avenue of horse chestnut trees leading to the church was absolutely bare, although there were still masses of golden leaves lying on the ground. My reason for visiting the church was to try and find the famous 'treacle well'. When I was young and heard people talking of Binsey treacle well, I thought, in my ignorance, that it was some sort of joke. (When we were children in Ducklington, we used to speak about Yelford pepper mills – Yelford being one of the loveliest and smallest villages in Oxfordshire, consisting of the manor house, a couple of farms, about six houses and a delightful little church; but, of course, there was never a pepper mill there, although we convinced a temporary school teacher from Lincolnshire that there was!) So, later on in life, I was pleased to find out that such a place as Binsey treacle well did exist, and that the word 'treacle' – in the

The Perch at Binsey, a favourite river-side inn

St Margaret's Well

St Margaret's church

medieval sense — was known as a healing fluid, and that Binsey had once belonged to Saint Frideswide's Priory.

Apparently, so the story goes, the origin of the healing well was brought about because St Frideswide — a consecrated nun — fled to Binsey to avoid the attentions of Algar, King of Leicester, who wished to marry her. He pursued her to Oxford but at the city gates he was struck blind. St Frideswide, on hearing of the tragedy, prayed for a healing well to spring from the earth near St Margaret's church and that the water should cure Algar's blindness, which — according to some reports — it did. The place then became a pilgrimage in the Middle Ages, and thousands of people flocked there seeking cures for their various ailments (some miracles were even performed there). The well and church is still visited by many people. On the day that I called there were just two young stone-masons repairing some of the stonework on the outside of the lovely, lonely little church. The interior, I noticed, was simply lit by oil lamps and candles. It was a quiet, peaceful place.

The treacle well, surrounded by pilgrims, can be seen in a stained-glass window in Christchurch Cathedral, and Lewis Carroll's *Alice in Wonderland* tells the story of three children who lived at the bottom of a treacle well. Apparently Lewis Carroll chose the Perch public house at Binsey for his first reading of the finished book.

I made my way back to Binsey, where I had arranged to meet Nick Elwes who lives at Weir Cottage on the banks of the Thames, which is about a quarter of a mile away from the village (just where the river divides — the left-hand side being the Medley, while the right-hand side the so-called

Isis). I first came to Bossoms boat-yard, where there were all sorts and types of boats; some were in the process of being done up, while others were awaiting the spring and summertime. I passed the beautiful rainbow bridge and arrived at Weir Cottage, and was soon sitting by a lovely wood-fire accompanied by Nick and his two dogs.

'Do you like crumpets?' Nick asked.

'Yes', I replied.

'Right', he said, 'we'll have some later when we've had a chat.'

Nick, I found out, has lived in Weir Cottage for the past eight years, and loves the river and Port Meadow and all its interesting aspects.

Permanent boats at Port Meadow, with the distant gleaming spires of Oxford

'Where do you get all your wood from?' I enquired, noticing a great stack of logs and uncut wood.

'When the river is in flood, it comes down by the ton, great logs and branches, so I get my boat out and yank as much as I can from the fast-flowing floods. I never buy any wood, there's no need of course.' And he went on, 'Do you realize that there are about 200 geese here on the meadow? I think some of them originated from the domestic ones that folk used to keep at Wolvercote, and they'd bring them on the meadow daily to graze. The geese are now known as 'Port Meadow Special'. I know a couple of fellows who thought they'd catch one: after a while they managed to collar one – then they wondered how they could get rid of their feathers. So, they tossed them on their indoor fire and – whoosh! – the draught took most of the feathers straight up the chimney, and they floated about outside.'

I meant to ask him if the geese were protected (thinking of the secrecy in trying to get rid of the feathers), for the story reminded me of the time when my grannie – who lived with my gramp on the Sherbourne estate in Gloucestershire – enticed a cock-pheasant into her hen run by sprinkling the ground with winey raisins – from her dandelion wine – for a week or more. By the end of that week the bird was really tiddly, and she easily caught him and rung his neck. When my gramp came home from work she excitedly told him what had happened, and that they were going to have the said bird for Sunday dinner. My gramp was furious; if the head keeper had got to hear of it, gramp would have been sacked on the spot, and they would be turned out of their tied lodge cottage.

'What yu going tu do with the bloody feathers?' he shouted.

'Burn 'um on a bonfire in the garden', she replied.

'Ah', he went on, red-faced and angry, 'What if the keeper smells the bloody feathers burning and comes asking – what yu goin'tu say then, eh?'

'Ah', my wise old gran replied, 'I'll just tell him I be burning an old cushion, what one of the grand-children piddled on.'

Nick went on, 'There's some funny things happen along here. One day a rowing boat containing eight fellows and a cox, came along – I think it must have been Eights Week – and these lads were in a very merry mood: they had probably won whatever event it was; they were in black-and-white gear. Anyway, they tied up their boat and wandered up to the Perch for a meal and a celebration. Very much later, as I was switching my outside light on – which I always do at night because I'd had a break-in or two – the young men were just on their way back, rowing along, laughing and singing merrily – and they were absolutely starkers!'

'Another time', Nick went on, between toasting crumpets on his lovely fire, 'A man – I think he was a retired station-master – used to come walking along here every day. Never said much, just "good morning". Anyhow, one day when he was passing some young louts who had ridden their bikes along Port Meadow, but had then chucked them down near the path and were teasing and cat-callin' to an old woman who was walking nearby. So he asked the boys to stop it – but they soon told him to "bug off", and called him a silly old man. He asked them again, but they just laughed in his face. At this, the usually quiet man, became annoyed and just caught hold of their bikes and threw them into the Thames, and coolly went off along the path, on with his walk.'

'Before you go', Nick said, 'You must see my outdoor privy' – knowing my interest in such things! He went on, 'It used to

The peewit, a visitor to Port Meadow

be a hopper type, now it's just an ordinary bucket sort. The contents are always sprinkled with sifted wood ash, which I sift from the wood fires. Then, when it goes on the garden – as of course it always does eventually – there's a goodly sprinkling of manure and potash, and I grow some wonderful crops.'

He had a copy of my book *Cotswold Privies* in the privy – 'just for guests to read while they are in there doing their bounden duty', he said, smiling.

Four or five young men in, what I think are called, single sculls (boats) were practising rowing on the river, with their instructor calling to them from the bank. We watched for a few minutes and then walked along to the rainbow bridge where Nick took his leave and crossed over to Port Meadow with his dogs.

Port Meadow was given to the citizens of Oxford by William the Conqueror as a free common, which it still is. It was a much larger area then, at least 500 acres, now it comprises about 342 acres. The common is a very popular place for walking, riding horses, and skating in winter-time, bird-watching and bathing. There were lots of horses on the common, and cattle, but sheep are not allowed. The meadow has never been ploughed up and is now a Site of Special Scientific Interest. One annual event is the drive by the Sheriff of Oxford across the meadow, which in some way helps to control the pasturing. Commoners and freemen have the right to let their animals graze on the meadow,

Port Meadow in winter

and can retrieve them for a nominal fee. However, if owners with no rights let their cattle roam on the meadow, then they are fined. All sorts of birds come there to feed and nest, and there are frequently many different winter visitors. Wild flowers also grow profusely, as does the dreaded ragwort! I remember that one year, when it was especially prolific, the authorities asked for volunteers to pull up the dreaded weed – cattle won't touch it as it is poisonous, and it spreads like wildfire if left to seed.

After days of rain, the weather changed suddenly to give clear windy days, with the pale winter sunshine too lazy to exude any warmth, but very welcome anyway.

And so I came to Osney, passing the lovely old church of St Frideswide on my right before I turned down into Osney proper. This was where the magnificent abbey of Osney once stood; it was built in

1287, but unfortunately destroyed – like so many others – by King Henry VIII in 1539. For centuries after, Osney was a quiet village separated from Oxford by the River Thames and the canal. Now it is a very busy place, with many large warehouses, and home to the *Oxford Mail*, *Oxford Times*, *Oxford Star* and the *Witney Gazette* newspapers. But there is still a country feeling about the place; a pair of swans flew low overhead, the sound of their wings was like the rustle of dry grasses, although someone once said that the sound was like an old man's wheezing chest! They settled gracefully on the river and set about looking for their dinner, heads down in the water, their rears in the air. Meanwhile a party of rooks tumbled about in the windy sky.

One of the beauties of wintertime is the leafless trees, with their topmost branches looking like fine filligree work. We don't see this loveliness at any other time of the year, but now every tree outlined against the pale blue sky is magical while the deep maroon-red branches of the dog-wood show up in contrast. The quiet road alongside the river is filled mostly with attractive Victorian cottages, but the road parallel to it

'Head of the River' inn

was quite busy as it leads to the offices and maintenance yard of the Thames Conservancy. This was where my old friend Ron May – about whom I wrote in the September chapter – started work in the 1950s, when there were still fields on the west side of the Conservancy 'yard'. He told me that during the winter months they would haul in the wooden boats, which were used on the Thames (or the Isis, as it is called where it flows through Oxford), for a number of things connected with work on the river. Well, these wooden boats would be turned upside-down and treated with a mixture of hot tar, pitch and cow pats, which they had to go out and gather in the nearby fields. This wondrous mixture helped to preserve and

Folly Bridge

seal the boats' sides and bottoms. And while at the time I thought this was funny, I found out later that this is, in fact, a recognized practice – to use cow dung; although one man I was talking to about this maintained that it was horse muck.

The walk along the tow-path to Folly Bridge was not very exciting and there was not much to see either, except for some rather pretty post-war houses and bungalows, their gardens filled with small shrubs, some in bloom. I think this would be a very pleasant place to live.

And so I arrived at Folly Bridge, once known as South Bridge or Grandpont, and crossed over to where a number of huge diesel-powered

View over the Thames to Oxford's lovely buildings

launches, belonging to Salters — the famous boat-builders who were apparently established in 1858 — were moored for wintertime. The wind had now died down, and the walk along the river here was most pleasant. In the distance many of the Oxford buildings — including some colleges — were edged against the winter sky, the buildings glowing gently in the pale early afternoon sunshine. In the foreground were the green and lovely meadows of Christchurch, while the chiming of distant bells from an Oxford church drifted across the almost still air. I walked along to where, at one time, many of the colourful university college barges were once moored — twenty-two to be exact. They belonged to the various colleges and were used by the boat crews as places to change their clothes, sit and drink tea and entertain their friends and families – who also used them as grandstands when the various activities took place there. Now, all these magnificent colourful barges have gone, although some of them are being restored nearby by a special preservation trust, so maybe we shall see some of them back once more on the river. In their place, however, but on the land nearby, a row of fairly modern boathouses have been built. I wonder if they have the same atmosphere as those lovely old ceremonial barges.

I walked back to Folly Bridge where the well-known Head of the River public house stands – so-called because the inn is close to the finishing line of the Torpids and Eights boat races, and where the winners become 'Head of the River'. According to a small booklet called *Tales of Ales*, produced by Oxford Marketing for Halls brewery, the inn is built on the site of a one-time old wharf. It also said that a rather tall red-brick building on the other side of the road opposite the inn (which I noticed had statues of ladies on almost every window ledge and a figure on the roof which looked remarkably like the devil!) was many years ago a *former* bordello, a house of ill repute!

It was, of course, because of journeys on the River Thames that the Revd Charles Dodgson, a lecturer at Christchurch College, wrote the wondrous tale of *Alice in Wonderland*, under the pseudonym of Lewis Carroll. The story developed from the trips he took on the river accompanied by the three daughters of Dean Liddell of Christchurch. Dodgson recalled the 'Golden afternoon that he started to tell the children . . . hungry for news of fairyland', who pleaded with him to tell them a story. The rest is history.

The river and canal at Oxford have, over the centuries, played a very important role, bringing goods, coal, stone and many other commodities from the Midlands and beyond. Now both river and canal are mostly used

Once *a house of 'ill repute'*

Magdalen Bridge, Oxford

for pleasure – the river no longer helps to drive the many mills that were dotted along its way. It is, of course, very much used by the university for innumerable boating events – notably the Torpids and May Eights – as well as for the training of crews for the famous boat races. The boat race crews also train at Wallingford, on the Thames, where there is a goodly stretch of water with no locks for six miles. Then, a couple of weeks before the boat race, the crew and their boat move to Putney. Of course, the beautiful city of Oxford is a must for any visitor, but there are already countless books on this subject, so I shall return to the river!

This time, I returned not to the Thames but to the Cherwell, which joins the Thames a little further along. But, before then, the river flows under the famous Magdalen Bridge – a favourite starting point for small craft and punts. On May Day the college choir sing on the top of Magdalen Tower at six o'clock in the morning, and scores of punts float by, laden with both male and female undergraduates, breakfasting on champagne and other wonderful things, the ladies dressed in their summer finery with flower-covered hats. A truly memorable occasion for them. And crowds of folk line the streets where groups of morris dancers perform. Well, it was here at Oxford that I intended to end my journey along the Thames, but I found out that nearby Iffley lock has for a long, long time, played an important role in the university boating calendar – so a few days later I made my way towards it.

It was absolutely tipping down with rain, but this was the only day I had to spare. On my way to the lock, I stopped by an old mill stone; in the wall near to it was a stone-carved plaque stating that for centuries a mill had stood there, but unfortunately it was destroyed by fire on 20 May 1908. Tony Sargent, the lock-keeper, who had been at Iffley for twenty-four years, was most helpful. He said that at one time the university boats which took part in the Torpids and May Eights races used to come right up to the lock to start off their rowing course.

'Where was that exactly?' I asked him.

'Oh, at the Bull ring', he replied.

'The bull ring', I thought. The mind boggled! The only bull ring that entered my head at that moment was the one in Birmingham. Seeing my puzzled expression, he smiled, and went on, 'Come along, and I'll show you.'

We walked towards a rather small, lovely stone bridge and there set in the wall nearby was a very handsome bull's head – copper, I thought it might be. It was situated below the old original Thames Common Seal of the Conservators.

'But where's the ring?' I enquired.

'Oh, some silly B—— pinched it some time ago – how the dickens they managed to force it out amazed me. But what the ring was used for was so that the cox in the boat could tie his boat up by threading the rope through the ring. Now', Tony went on, 'the university boats are not allowed to come up this far because one year, apparently, the river was a bit high and rough and some of the boats got into the fast stream which was taking them towards the weir. They did manage to right their craft but it could have been very serious, and after that the start of the Torpids and May Eights races take place further down the river, near to the Isis Hotel.'

I turned to look at the small ornamental bridge. It is called Desborough Bridge after Lord Desborough who was a conservator of the Thames and who, incidentally, opened this newly built lock here at Iffley in 1923.

Tony went on, 'The idea of this bridge over a small side stream – which, of course, *is* part of the river – is so that punts and small craft can go

Lovely Desborough Bridge at Iffley

through; then — see those rollers in front? — well, having come under the bridge they then haul their boats up those rollers and finally make it to the main river, thereby bypassing the lock.

As I left, I saw a stone plaque which stated that in 1632 the first *pound* lock was built there (and some bits of it still remain). Pound locks were mostly owned by the land owners and the like, who also owned the river where it ran through their land. They demanded fees from the passing boats that were carrying all sorts of things. If no fee was available, then the boat was *impounded* until such times as the fee was paid — well, that was the story I was told anyway!

So, with the rain still coming down like stair-rods, I ended my Thames journey as I had begun it, in January — in the pouring rain, but with some glorious summer days in between.

The seal of Thames Water Authority

The Old Waterman

And so, Eights Week is coming round again.
I think I'll take a stroll beside the river.
The sky looks all the bluer for the rain.

The smell of may hangs heavy by the Plain
And sets an old man's memories a-quiver
To think Eights Week is coming round again.

Time was I knew them all, the rowing men.
Boy-like I thought them gods, the great and clever.
As skies look all the bluer for the rain

So rowing shows a man his proper grain,
Swinging and sweating in a crew together.
Ah well— And so Eights Week is round again.

Mind you, it's naught to what it was. But then
What is? Things can't go on the same for ever.
The sky looks all the bluer for the rain.

Storms pass and men. But the real things remain,
The shouts, the lungs pumped dry, the gasped endeavour,
The bump! And hark! Eights Week is here again.
The sky looks all the bluer for the rain.

Maida Stanier
The New Oxford Spy

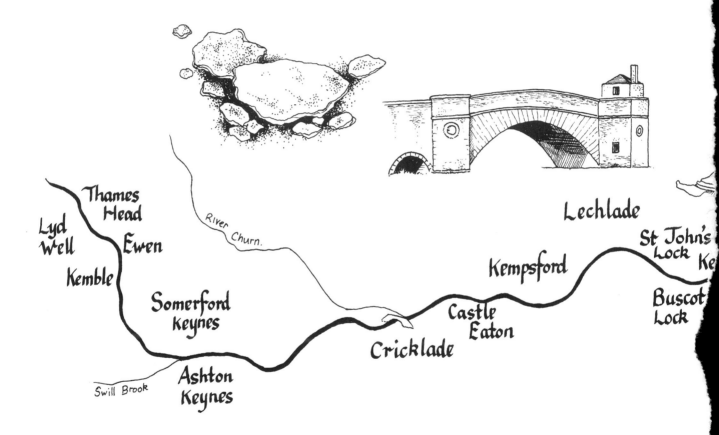

Thames
Head

Lyd
Well   Ewen

River Churn.

Kemble

Lechlade

Somerford
Keynes

Kempsford   St John's
Lock
Ke

Castle
Eaton   Buscot
Lock

Swill Brook   Ashton
Keynes   Cricklade

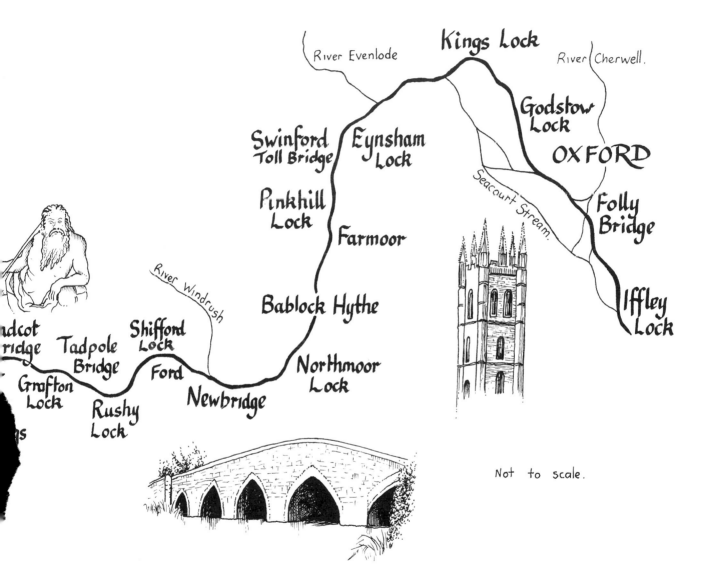

River Evenlode

Kings Lock

River Cherwell.

Swinford
Toll Bridge

Eynsham
Lock

Godstow
Lock

OXFORD

Pinkhill
Lock

Farmoor

Seacourt Stream.

Folly
Bridge

River Windrush

Bablock Hythe

Iffley
Lock

dcot
ridge

Tadpole
Bridge

Shifford
Lock

Grafton
Lock

Ford

Northmoor
Lock

Rushy
Lock

Newbridge

as

Not to scale.